With every
wish from the Author -

Michael Green

The Art of Coarse Sex

MICHAEL GREEN

The Art of Coarse Sex

*or How to Love Better and Die with a
Beautiful Smile on Your Face*

Hutchinson
London Melbourne Sydney Auckland Johannesburg

Hutchinson & Co. (Publishers) Ltd

An imprint of the Hutchinson Publishing Group

3 Fitzroy Square, London W1P 6JD

Hutchinson Group (Australia) Pty Ltd
30-32 Cremorne Street, Richmond South, Victoria 3121
PO Box 151, Broadway, New South Wales 2007

Hutchinson Group (NZ) Ltd
32-34 View Road, PO Box 40-086, Glenfield, Auckland 10

Hutchinson Group (SA) Pty Ltd
PO Box 337, Bergvlei 2012, South Africa

First published 1981
© Michael Green 1981

Illustrations © Hutchinson & Co. Ltd 1981
Set in Linoterm Baskerville

Printed in Great Britain by The Anchor Press Ltd
and bound by Wm Brendon & Son Ltd,
both of Tiptree, Essex
British Library Cataloguing in Publication Data
Green, Michael
    The art of coarse sex.
    1. Sex – Anecdotes, facetiae, satire, etc.
    I. Title
    301.41'7'0207   HQ23

ISBN 0 09 144860 3

To Sir Clifford Chatterley,
a man

Contents

Acknowledgements

I am very grateful to all the people who have helped to provide material for this book. I shall not embarrass them by printing their names, especially as I have forgotten some of them (frequently when saying goodbye in the morning). But thank you just the same.

Author's Warning

In previous books in the Coarse series I have felt it advisable to issue a warning about the dangers of readers injuring themselves by taking the so-called advice. This followed a distressing incident on a golf course when a player attempted to follow one of the strokes described in *The Art of Coarse Golf* and dislocated his shoulder. Another tried a cocktail recipe from *The Art of Coarse Drinking* and nearly poisoned his wife. I don't think I need stress the point as regards *The Art of Coarse Sex*, except to say that, if you must swing from the chandelier, don't blame me if the lights fuse. Genuine advise can always be obtained from the Marriage Guidance Council, whether you're married or not.

MICHAEL GREEN

1 An Introduction to Coarse Sex

The position is ridiculous; the pleasure momentary; and the expense damnable.   THE EARL OF CHESTERFIELD

In praise of sex's forgotten man – terrible experience on football field – pressures of society – why everybody lies about sex – what happened to the hotel receptionist – Askew's dreadful honeymoon night – a simple Coarse Sex quiz

A friend of mine was telling me the other day how he had an affair with a girl student in his university days. It was summer, so for their first weekend together they went camping on bicycles and when night fell they snuggled happily together among the deserted sand dunes of the east coast. They started to make love but their passionate movements disturbed the tentpole and the whole thing fell down on top of them. As my friend put it, 'It was easier to re-erect the tent than me,' but eventually both of them fell together once more in passion. Suddenly they jumped apart with terrible cries of pain. 'Bloody hell!' shouted the man. 'The damn contraceptive's full of sand.'

That was the end of the lovemaking. Next morning they painfully cycled back to college.

I tell this story because it illustrates what I mean by Coarse Sex. That is why this book is dedicated to Sir Clifford Chatterley, husband of Lady Chatterley, and not to his wife. As the athletic heroine of D. H. Lawrence's classic *Lady Chatterley's Lover*, and the universal symbol of passionate love, she would seem to have the better claim, since Sir Clifford's sexual activities were restricted by his being confined to a wheelchair with wartime injuries, while his wife had an unceasing sexual orgy with the gamekeeper. But I have chosen Sir Clifford, not because his french letters were full of sand, but because, like Coarse Lovers, he found his sex life wasn't quite on that high plane which we are told it should be.

As those who have read other books in this series will know, the Coarse approach to a subject is the way it happens in real life as opposed to the theoretical way of doing it. Coarse in this connection has nothing to do with crudeness but with stark, unrefined reality. Thus your textbook yachtsman never twitches an eyebrow in a crisis but calmly orders the course to be changed four points to port. In *The Art of Coarse Sailing*, however, I point out that a Coarse Sailor would forget nautical language and shout, 'For God's sake turn left!' And, while all the textbooks portray rugby players as human giants impervious to pain or fear, we all know that 75 per cent are much more likely to be shivering sales representatives plodding around a manure-covered field in the suburbs and avoiding physical danger as much as possible.

So it is in life as in sport. The majority of us are hacking our way painfully round the golf course of existence only hoping that the game is going to last the full eighteen holes and that the great club secretary in the sky won't object to the damage we've done to the turf.

It is interesting to note, by the way, that as the man in the wheelchair can symbolize Coarse Sex so he can also typify Coarse Sport. For years I played in a rugby side which was actually captained by a man in a wheelchair. He was a former skipper recovering from a serious car crash and he refused to give up the captaincy, leading the side from the touchline by shouting and waving his arms. Unfortunately, he deliberately drove his wheelchair in front of an opponent who was about to score and he had to be banned from the ground.

Not that Coarse Lovers are as helpless as a man in a wheelchair (although sometimes they may be). But these days it's only too easy for anyone to feel they've fallen below par. In the same way that sportsmen are pressurized to believe losing is the unforgivable sin so we're all expected to keep up to scratch sexually. It's a world of the glossy magazine the sex manual and the sex symbol, whose heroes, such as James Bond, can summon up an erection at the drop of a hat, even underwater if necessary. It is a world where everyone enjoys it all the time, and if they don't there's something wrong with them, and where the sordid side of sex (like your partner's rotting feet) is never mentioned. It bears about as much relation to real life as the Open Championship does to a meeting of the office golf society.

Sometimes the fiction may be reality. But ordinary mortals are often playing in the second division of sex, the third team of love as it were. When I told a woman neighbour I was writing this book she said, 'Yes, I know what you mean by Coarse Sex all right. It's when your husband comes home from the match on Saturday nights half pissed and reeking of curry, and wants to have it away as soon as he's opened the door, and then finds he can't.'

Women's magazines used to advise girls to resist their boyfriend's desire to sleep with them. But for years now they've been on the sex bandwagon and anxious girls write:

I am very worried as I cannot have multiple orgasms. My boyfriend is also worried as *he* cannot have multiple orgasms. He tried to, but the room kept spinning round. Sometimes he can only do it four times a night and he thinks it might be his fault. What is wrong with us? Desperate, Slough.

There's no escape from the stream of stuff urging us on. There's a whole literary sex industry bombarding us with medical case histories like this:

CASE OF THE UNDER-SEXED LABOURER:
AN INTERESTING CURE

John was a fifty-five-year-old farm labourer who had been married for twenty-five years and had twelve children. He worked thirteen hours a day and was rarely home before eight in the evening. His wife came to my clinic and complained that recently he had taken to covering her face with an old potato sack during intercourse. Lovemaking now took place only on public holidays and then at her request. She asked if anything was wrong with her husband and if she was losing her attractiveness. After carefully questioning her, and discovering her husband did not have a potato fetish, I suggested she took the sack herself, cut holes for eyes, nose and mouth, embroidered it with pink ribbon and Valentine motifs, and called it her love mask. She did so and hung it on the end of the bed. Now, when she wants her husband to make love to her, she puts it over her face and says shyly, 'How do you like me in my love mask?' Their sexual life is fully restored, although the husband has lost his job at the farm as he can't get up in the mornings.

This, then, is the crazy world in which the Coarse Lover must survive. It might help to define a Coarse Lover, but it isn't easy. One thing that does distinguish him is his eternal optimism. No sexual experience is so vile as to put him off trying again. He's also rather nostalgic, and always harking back to a supposed romantic past with phrases such as, 'She was the girl I really should have married.' Perhaps it's best to define a Coarse Lover as one who always hopes it will be better next time or one who always believes it *was* better last time. Another way of putting it is to say a Coarse Lover is one who suspects other people are getting more out of their sex lives than he is. In fact, his love life is probably no worse than many and better than some, but he won't believe that.

I say 'he' because, although a lot of what I say might apply to women, I haven't the audacity to pretend to be able to speak from their point of view. Nature has disqualified me from that (despite the comment of a girlfriend who said mysteriously, 'I think life would have been a lot easier for you, Mike, if you had been a lesbian.') So I talk from the male point of view not out of prejudice but because I am not a woman. The female cause has been pleaded by better pens than mine.

The first thing to accept in the world of Coarse Sex is that truth flies out of the door when sex is mentioned. Does anyone ever give the *real* reasons for a break-up? It's usually some sweet rationalization about both of them being too keen on their careers, not his habit of trying to make love at breakfast with his mouth full of cornflakes while she was washing the dishes.

It is said the three great lies of life are: 1 'The cheque's in the post.' 2 'This may hurt a little when the injection wears off.' 3 'I swear I'll withdraw in time.' But in Coarse Sex there are so many others. One of the greatest is the fantasy 'I had the hotel receptionist.' If every man who claimed to have made love to the hotel receptionist was telling the truth, then nobody would have been able to book a hotel room in Britain for the last twenty years, as the desk staff would have all been flat on their backs satisfying the lusts of the customers. An associated boast is that of the Mile High Club, whose members allege they have made love in aircraft or seduced air stewardesses in flight. I have never discovered where these affairs took place. In a seat with the other passengers all smiling at the happy pair? Or standing up in that little pantry where they heat the food with the cabin staff pushing by and saying, 'Excuse me, old chap, can I get at the breakfast?' Funnily enough, I went out with an air stewardess and was once on the same flight as her, so I had the opportunity to join the club and I still couldn't think of anywhere to qualify for membership. A friend says a deserted first-class cabin at night on a long haul is the place. I'll believe that when I can afford to travel first class.

Closely allied to these fantasies is the Great Public Place Boast, in which the speaker brags of the bizarre places in which he has had sex. I have listened to men who have claimed to have managed it during a college lecture, in the cinema, or in a lift between the basement and the top floor (either a slow lift or a very tall building, presumably). I also knew a man who claimed to have had sexual intercourse during a cricket match. 'I was fielding on the boundary,' he said, 'and I got chatting to this girl and we hopped over the hedge at the end of the over. Nobody noticed until they hit a ball where I should have been fielding, then they all made such a row I had to run back pulling up my trousers.' A likely tale.

A friend of mine in Birmingham is a sex maniac. Well, perhaps not in the conventional sense, but he can't talk of anything else. He is one of those Great Sex Bores and, if you travel in a car with him, he treats the passengers to a guided tour of places where he's made love: 'See that house? I used to go out with a nurse who lived there . . . passionate beyond belief she was . . . I wonder the house is still standing. . . . Now that's a very interesting park on the left. I once had my boss's secretary in there. During the lunch hour by that clump of bushes. You can still see the impression in the soil if you look closely. . . . Ah, now that alleyway on the right could tell a tale. I got a grope there in 1972 . . . and I had it off on that empty site across the road . . . lovely girl, half Chinese. You see that little grocery shop over there . . . got a bit of teat in the doorway going home from a dance once . . . never forget it. . . .'

Now there is an example of what a sex-orientated society does to a man.

One of the most menacing fantasies is the cry, 'I know a club where there's lots of women.' This is frequently raised by some know-all on sporting tours and business trips and is invariably followed by disaster. I write bitterly as one who fell for this line in Norwich on a wet Tuesday evening at 11.30 p.m. I don't know if any readers have walked around Norwich looking for sex on a wet Tuesday evening but it wasn't a pleasant experience, especially when it took half an hour to find the haunt of sin and five pounds to get in – only to find there wasn't a girl in the place except for a couple of middle-aged waitresses knitting. I don't blame Norwich. The same thing happened to me in Brussels.

That didn't stop our guide claiming next morning to those who hadn't gone that it had been a night of unparalleled lust. 'You should have seen Mike, he got two of them,' he said tapping his nose and leering. That's another aspect of sex: no one is allowed to be honest about failure. It was no use saying I had been nowhere near any girl; they all chorused, 'Tell us another one.' In the end it's easier to lie. It's all part of the great game.

I shan't forget my friend Askew having an explosion of sexual fantasy when drunk at one of his own dinner parties. As he slowly sank below the table he claimed to have made love five times in one night.

'Five?' repeated his wife bitterly. 'His record is one and a half. And even then he was like our old Morris Minor and had to be started up by hand.' She never did explain what the half was.

Drink, of course, is a great stimulator of Coarse Sex fantasies, but it can also encourage truth. My experience is that, after two drinks, everyone is saying how good they are at it, but if you persevere for ten more whiskies all sorts of embarrassing confidences come forth, such as 'Between you and me old man, I don't enjoy it any more.' Never take up the speaker on his confidences next day or he will deny them. 'Rubbish, old chap, we do it all the time. I never said anything like that.'

Let's take my friend Askew again ('Yes, take him right away,' says his wife). Both he and his wife have frequently referred in lurid detail to their honeymoon fifteen years ago yet their descriptions are in complete opposition. I will first give the wife's version verbatim, as related to me when she called round last week to return a book.

ASKEW'S HONEYMOON NIGHT
as told by Sheila Askew

'Our honeymoon night? I must have told you dozens of times about that. I suppose you want it for that filthy book of yours, although how you can think anything as sordid as that can be of public interest defeats me. . . . Yes, thanks . . . not too much tonic, it drowns the gin . . . but anyway, as long as you promise not to use my name, I'll tell you again.* Well, in those days, what with there being no pill and everything, plenty of girls came to their bridal nights as virgins, technically at least, assuming you don't count those furtive gropes in the car by the golf course. This wasn't anything to do with virtue; it was largely because we were afraid of having babies and because at school they'd told us we would go to Hell if we Did It, not to mention catching VD. Actually I'd have been quite prepared to let old Jack have it off before, but his attitude to birth control was so bloody casual – rather like his attitude to work – that I was scared stiff something would go wrong, so young Sheila reports for duty on the marriage night comparatively pure. Well, I need hardly tell you that Jack was pissed at the wedding. Absolutely and completely shotters, and he didn't stop all evening – yes, not so much tonic in it this time . . . ice, lovely – and, talk about the impatient bridegroom, we didn't get to bed

---

* Sorry. I always was a rat.

until nearly midnight. To this day I don't know what really happened. I felt a sort of groping, as if an elderly octopus was trying to interfere with me and then suddenly he rolled over and fell asleep, snoring and breaking wind gently.

'I lay awake thinking, "Am I still a virgin?" and being unable to make up my mind. Three times in the night Jack woke up and I lay quivering with anticipation but twice he went for a pee and once to be sick and then he fell asleep again. In the morning he woke up looking extremely sorry for himself and tottered to the suitcase and brought out a bottle of beer, which he drank in one go. He said he always had a glass first thing in the morning. A nice time to find out your husband's revolting habits I must say. And that was our honeymoon night. It took him two more nights to achieve what I believe is technically known as penetration and then only because to stimulate him I descended to what my old vicar would have called bestial practices. Now listen, Mike Green, just you promise not to print any of this or I will never speak to you again – yes . . . just one more gin and then I must go. . . .'

Askew's own story is somewhat different:

ASKEW'S HONEYMOON NIGHT
As described by Jack Askew

'I kid you not, old chap. I very nearly injured myself in a vital part. Five times . . . yes, five times I gave young Sheila Askew the old going-over. She couldn't get enough of it. They're all the same these upper-middle-class girls, get 'em away from Mummy and Daddy and they go at it like rabbits – funny thing, old man, my glass has suddenly emptied itself. Yes, I could take a shot more Scotch . . . a decent one this time, if you don't mind, not a smear in the bottom of the glass. Now where was I? Ah, yes . . . in the end Sheila had to beg me to stop. The fact is I find whisky a wonderful aphrodisiac, and I'd had a skinful at the wedding, as you know. I could have gone on all night.

'But here's the astonishing thing. As Sheila was lying in bed exhausted, with a contented smile on her face, I took a run

before breakfast – I have this thing about fitness, you know –
and as I trotted downstairs in my tracksuit the receptionist
smiled at me. Young thing, about twenty. And I tell you
without a word of a lie, old chap, I had her . . . no, not
immediately – during the lunch hour when Sheila was resting
again. And that isn't the end of the story, old son. Four days
later I was alone in the bedroom when the chambermaid came
in to make the bed, and I had her too. I speak not with forked
tongue. . . .'

But can poor Askew be blamed when every hero of popular
literature is a sexual giant? I have just read a spy thriller in
which the hero was trapped in a mountain hut with enemies
closing in all round. They have sworn to kill him unpleasantly.
So the hero takes the girl he is with and makes love to her and
(as the book put it) 'He was young and lusty and it lasted a long
time and it was good.'

If anyone really thinks it is going to be good with a sub-
machine-gun poking round the door, they are unacquainted
with the facts of life. Yet this sort of thing sets our sexual
standards. I can only say my own sense of guilt is so highly
developed that a knock on the door from the postman is enough
to render me useless, let alone a sub-machine-gun.

It is some consolation that an analysis of most thriller heroes
reveals that in real life they would be inclined to impotence
rather than performance. The obsession with guns and violence, the streak of cruelty, the love of fast cars, the inability to
establish a permanent relationship, are all significant. So is the
desire to have it off in a mountain hut surrounded by armed
killers.

To understand better what is meant by Coarse Sex I have
devised a simple little quiz. Readers are invited to answer the
questions below as honestly as they dare and then refer to the
answers at the end of the quiz, together with the ratings for the
various answers.

Perhaps I should say at once that I always distrust these
quizzes myself. Whenever I answer those about drinking, for
instance, I finish up with a score that proves I am a raving

alcoholic. For example: Do you crave for a drink during the day? – Yes; Do you drink at lunchtime? – Yes; Do you feel unhappy when you do not have a drink? – Yes; Do you drink alone? – Yes; and so forth. In the same way sex questionnaires always give me a score which reveals me as a pitiful, distorted creature, the slave of my own lusts: Would you make love to a girl even if you were not in love with her? – Yes; Would you make love to a girl just for one night? – Yes; etc. Nevertheless, the answers may prove something. I'm not quite sure what.

THE COARSE SEX QUIZ
(scores at the end)

1   Have you ever made love with your hat on?
2   Have you ever experienced a strong sexual desire on a bus? Or *for* a bus for that matter? (Older readers may substitute tram.)
3   Has a woman ever nicknamed you Flash Harry?
4   Does your partner smoke during intercourse?
5   Has your partner ever tried to leave the room while you were making love? (Note: If insertion has taken place, this can be dangerous.)
6   Have you ever woken up in the morning and said to yourself, 'Never again'?
7   Has your lovemaking ever been mistaken for foreplay?
8   Have you ever experienced a warm glow after making love?
9   Has your partner ever laughed just as you were about to have an orgasm?
10 Have you ever wished you were having a drink with the lads just as you were making love to a girl?
11 Have you ever paid for sex?
12 Has a woman ever talked unceasingly during the entire sex act?
13 Has a woman ever asked, 'Have you started yet?' just as you were finishing?
14 Have you ever made love to a woman who was reading the *Guardian*?
15 Did she stop reading?

16 Has a woman ever complained of feeling sick after you have had intercourse?

17 Has your partner ever made love with *her* hat on?

18 Have the neighbours ever complained?

ANSWERS

Score one point for each yes with the exception of the following:

 8 Only when the house was on fire.

11 We all pay one way or the other.

15 No.

RATINGS

Score of 16 points or over: I think you should seek help. Or something. Or someone. Don't come to me.

Over 10. Join the club. You are a Coarse Lover.

Over 5. You are the sort of well-adjusted person I can't stand, because they are so happy.

Below 5. Is your name Mellors by any chance?

2 Early Days or What Happened on the Barbed Wire

The headmaster never expels, except for beastlines... KIPLING, *Stalky and Co.*

Sex and the young – unpleasant incident at lunch – Oscar for VD film – making love to a barbed wire fence – tragedy in the snow – they should tell us about these things

Today's young people are luckier than many previous generations in as much as they are usually encouraged at school to think of sex as something normal, whereas most of their elders were brought up to think of it as something furtive and forbidden. However, I am still willing to warrant that the careful lectures, slides and diagrams of wriggling sperms still mean less to the modern child than playground gossip ('They say that if you do it before you're fifteen you go blind in one eye. . . .').

At my old school, more years ago than I care to remember, the fifth form were assembled once a year in the Great Hall, with its cavernous echoes and rolls of honour from the wars, and were subjected to a lecture on sex which by today's standards would appear quite ludicrous. In those times, however, it was considered rather advanced. It's a sign of how inhibited we were that, although we were supposed to ask our parents for permission to hear the lecture, we were all too embarrassed even to mention it.

The lecture was given by the headmaster, a fearsome figure with a mane of white hair and a gown and mortar board, who would sweep on to the platform, cough in an embarrassed manner, and begin with the time-honoured opening, 'Boys. . . .' There was then a pause while he collected his courage, since he was even more embarrassed by the whole thing than we were, and then he would launch forth.

'Boys . . . I have called you here today to tell you how you were born,' he would begin. We all stirred in anticipation but this promise of explicitness was not fulfilled. Instead, he rambled on for a long time about the birds, the flowers, and the love of man for a maid, while the louts of the fifth form grew restless and waited for him to get to the nitty-gritty. At length, the promised moment arrived.

'Boys . . . you have noticed certain changes taking place in your young bodies [muttered cries of 'You don't say, guv?']. Hair may be found growing in certain places . . . such as the armpits. . . . You may feel a vague restlessness for which you cannot account. This is because Nature is preparing you for the act of procreation. . . .'

At this point his nerve would fail and he would skate round the act of love by describing it in vague terms such as 'the union of man and woman . . . ultimate union, if I may use the term . . . a mystical communion in which your wife is the counterpart of you. . . .' With feeble gestures his voice trailed away.

This furiously irritated his listeners because what we wanted to know was the thousand-dollar question: How Do You Do It? The sheer physical implications were beyond our imaginations, in the absence of any reliable information other than playground gossip, since we had only the vaguest idea of what the female reproductive organs looked like. The whole thing seemed so ludicrous we couldn't imagine our parents ever having behaved like that.

However, leaving our curiosity unsatisfied, the headmaster swiftly skated on to safer ice. Sexual desire was treated as something unhealthy, and if it came on we were advised to wrestle or go for a bicycle ride (a voice from the back: 'How do you ride a bicycle with an erection, guv?'). The head was much more at home denouncing 'filthy practices', on which he blamed the bad examination results and the poor record of the First XI. Unfortunately, we weren't quite sure what he meant but we all felt duly guilty. We then sang a hymn entitled 'Keep Thyself Pure' and departed, little the wiser, to continue our sex education in furtive groups in the playground.

Yet, even today, sex education is still a problem. One teacher showed me a book which said, 'When mummy and daddy want to make a baby they do a special type of wriggling.' Another complained bitterly of a TV sex film 'showing a picture of someone's arse going up and down while a choir sang heavenly music. It had the sixth form in fits.' Today's sex education is probably years behind the children's experience.

Perhaps the Japanese had the best idea with their pillow book. Many years ago, newly-wed couples used to find a scroll under their pillow telling them how to make love and they were supposed to sit up in bed and read it together, and then apply the instructions ('It says here, honourable wife lie on back while unworthy husband crawl on top. . . .').

Mind you, there are still hazards in bringing up children in an uninhibited way. I know one rather trendy couple who refuse to let their children call their private parts by jolly euphemisms such as 'my little winky'; they insist on using the medical terms and discuss sex with the children as if they were adults. Fine in theory, but at a recent Sunday lunch one of the kids, aged about nine, suddenly piped up, 'Mummy, do you like it when daddy puts his male organ in your vagina?' Not to be outdone, his younger brother added, 'Yes, and do you ever get stuck together like those two doggies did?' Somehow, conversation rather flagged after that. Mummy did not answer the questions.

For many of my generation, sex education was continued in the forces, but the army's concern was not moral welfare, but simply to prevent VD. It was easily the best entertainment of the week and consisted either of gory lectures from the medical officer or the showing of films made for American troops. These were far more exciting than the Hollywood rubbish at the camp cinema. They usually had a small plot, inevitably about a group of soldiers going down town on a Saturday night and all becoming diseased. Sometimes they went to a brothel ('Is mah favourite, Lucy Belle, here tonight, ma'am?' 'She sho is, and rarin' to go, sah.') The film then showed their subsequent infection in some detail, plus interesting shots of female symptoms, and ended with the VD-stricken soldiers being manacled while we all cheered heartily. There was a hoary myth about one VD film so gruesome that everyone fainted ('And we're being shown that next week.') We never were.

Another myth was that Russian troops had contracted a form of VD so strong it was impervious to any known drugs except a bullet, which was rumoured to be the normal Soviet cure. 'It's because they're from Central Asia,' said the barrack-room lawyer. 'Ever since Ghengis Khan they've had a special virulent strain there. He were a dirty bugger were that there Ghengis Khan.'

Strangely enough, however, the first and most sensible piece of sex education I ever received was in the army. We had a corporal named Tug Wilson who was being pursued by a young girl who was nuts about him. I asked Tug why he didn't take advantage of the fact. 'Because,' he said simply, 'my cock belongs to my wife. That's what they call marriage, son.' I have yet to hear a better summing-up of sexual morality.

Incidentally, the American obsession with VD even penetrated their record request programmes on forces radio. While the British would be relaying a talk on farming, American programmes were punctuated with, 'Remember soldier! VD walks the streets! Keep sober, keep clean! And now back to Benny Goodman. . . .' No wonder we always listened to the US Radio Gorizia (the Voice of The Blue Devils, 88th Division — the Kraut Killers, as they modestly styled themselves).

The trouble with sex education is that it doesn't prepare you for the fact that early experiences are usually rather sordid and furtive. So are plenty of later experiences, for that matter. My old Uncle Walter claims his first taste of love was on the back seat of an empty upper deck of a Midland Red bus travelling between Leicester and Birmingham, but I suspect this is another of those public place fantasies, the 1938 equivalent of the Mile High Club. But I can say in all honesty, my own first experience was unusual, because I contracted a frostbitten penis.

Like most of my generation I matured late, and was nineteen and a soldier before it happened. Up to then my activities had been confined to attempts at undoing girls' blouses in the cinema. An earlier assault on the citadel of sex some months before had failed. An army friend and myself had gone to a brothel in Italy with the intention of losing our innocence properly and sat down in a large waiting room with thirty other soldiers. With three rooms in constant use and a five-minute time limit, the queue moved swiftly. Just before our turn a drunken and diseased-looking Canadian soldier lurched out of one room with a girl, buttoning up his trousers and loudly exclaiming, 'Gee, that was some shag.' The girl then adjusted her knickers and minced over to my friend Ginger, and clawed at Ginger's loins by way of invitation. It was too much for a couple of well-brought-up young lads and we fled, pursued by the mocking shouts of the girls.

However, we shortly moved to Germany where my innocence was ended by a girl I met at a regimental dance. I never knew her name or even her nationality and our brief conversation was in broken German. She came from a local refugee camp and I think she was probably Russian as her name sounded like something out of *Dr Zhivago*. She shared a hut with thirty other refugees so we had to consummate our passion out of doors and that bitter February night the temperature sank to minus 27 degrees centigrade according to the thermometer outside the guardroom.

It was so cold that anti-freeze froze in the trucks. No wonder my unhappy organ also froze. The deed was done furtively against the barbed wire fence surrounding the camp and, as soon as I had struggled with those special army trouser buttons that won't undo, a blast of icy air numbed my sensitive parts. As I attempted to perform the act my feet slid from under me on the frozen ground and I fell flat on my face. I struggled upright, cursing and swearing, and managed to keep my balance by hanging on to the barbed wire until it was all over, when I fell down again and this time my long-suffering member went into a pile of snow. So much for the 'mystic communion' of which the headmaster had spoken. I do feel that he, in common with other sex lecturers, could have said something more practical. I handed over some cigarettes to the girl to buy food, and fled back to barracks.

Here, further trouble awaited me. A soldier intending to make love was required to collect a contraceptive and some protective cream to be used before intercourse. Afterwards he had to spend an hour going through an anti-VD obstacle course, urinating in gushes, anointing the parts with anti-septic and scrubbing his loins. After all this, it's a miracle anyone bothered to make love at all. Many didn't. However, on this night there was no hot water and I had to break an icicle off the tap before scrubbing. Small wonder when I'd finished my member had no feeling in it and the end turned blue. It was no better next morning, so I paraded before the medical officer.

The odd thing about the MO was that he couldn't bring himself to say the word 'penis'. 'Now look here, Green,' he said, addressing me in that tone of talking to a half-wit which army officers favoured in those days, 'this is a damn bad show, getting your little whurlitzer in this state. I've never seen anything like it. What would happen to the army if we all got our whurlitzers like this, eh?'

However, he treated my frozen little whurlitzer, but when I recovered I was in no hurry to repeat the experiment until warmer weather had come. Even today I feel a sense of dread when the bedclothes become disarranged and a cold draught blows across my loins. I instinctively protect myself and my partner will say, 'Why are you clutching your balls so closely? I know you're old, but surely they won't fall off in the night?'

The story is typical of the first experiences of love, which are frequently hasty consummations in unsuitable places, even if they don't always lead to frostbite, and which rarely have any relation to that mystic communion between man and woman of which we hear so much. All too often, the first time is Coarse Sex. The trouble with the Coarse Lover is that the same sort of thing is liable to happen throughout the rest of his life.

3 How to Attract Women

Men are April when they woo,
December when they wed.
SHAKESPEARE (*As You Like It*)

*Difficulties of getting women – difficulties of fighting them off –
enormous cost of courtship – wheezes to attract the wenches – irrationality
of female sex – Askew's terrible experience*

It never ceases to surprise me that, in the vital matter of the
sexes getting together, Nature has arranged things so badly.
Most men would agree life would be simpler if it was socially
acceptable to go up to a girl who was attractive to you and ask
her to make love. Alas, it isn't, and I do know the stories about
men who go around saying that to every girl and who get a lot of
refusals but a lot of successes as well, but those are other male
fantasies. The only man I knew who genuinely did that was
suffering from a severe personality disorder and on the few
occasions a girl said yes he ran away in panic. Eventually he was
arrested for exposing himself at a dance.

However, we must accept life as it is, as they'll tell you in the
mental home, and if Nature has designed the human mating
process to be complicated there's nothing to do but fit into the
pattern. Animals, too, have complicated courtship routines.
Monkeys stand on their heads or something similar. Foxes go
through a sort of dance in which they wave their tails over each
other. A fox who marches up to a vixen and asks her to jump
into the nearest burrow will get nowhere. Some insects actually
die after the mating process, and I must say I've felt the same
way myself sometimes. A man, too, has to go through a ritual
which may involve going to places he doesn't want to visit and

seeing films he doesn't want to see and meeting people he doesn't want to know. The same applies to women, of course.

A pale of mine once met a girl who worked in a theatre ticket agency. Thinking she must be interested in the stage, he affected a similar interest and took her round several shows. It was a whirlwind romance and they married within a few weeks, and he suggested they might spend their honeymoon at the Edinburgh Festival. The first day there they saw three plays. The first was totally incomprehensible and nobody knew when it had finished; in the second the actors went round abusing the audience; and the third began with three little heaps of vomit on the stage. On the next day they went to a lunchtime show. The lights went up on a man tied to a grand piano. Then a lot of women came in and began to kick him in the groin to the accompaniment of weird music. My pal looked at his bride and thought she looked bored so he asked her, 'Are you sure you want to see this?'

'No,' she replied, 'but I thought *you* did.'

It transpired that neither of them was interested in the avant-garde theatre but both had the impression the other was. They immediately left the hall, went into a pub and spent the rest of the honeymoon in various bars.

A great paradox of sex is that the more you try the less you succeed with women, and vice versa, although that's true of other areas of life as well. It's absolute rubbish that, as women's magazines used to allege, one can conquer a girl by sending her flowers, or whispering sweet nothings in her ear by candlelight. I've tried it. And it doesn't work, unless the girl wants you anyway, in which case you needn't have bothered. If a woman doesn't want a man she won't have him, not even if he sends her a parkful of flowers. She'll just accept the gifts and say, 'I look upon you as a real friend. Don't let's spoil it all by having an affair.' (I never understand how women can talk of making love as 'spoiling it', but that's by the way.)

Talking of the alleged romantic effect of soft lighting and so forth, my old Uncle Walter takes the opposite view.

'Far from soft lights being any use, my boy,' he told me, 'the antithesis is true. The finest piece of lovemaking I ever indulged in was against the wall of Southwold Lighthouse when I was in the RAF during the war. Every five seconds we were completely blinded by a dazzling glare and then plunged into darkness. It had an incredible effect on the girl. Far from all this stuff about dim lights and soft music I would advise a young man who wants an interesting experience to court his girlfriend under floodlights, preferably with an air raid going on at the same time. An explosion brings on the girl wonderfully.'

On the other hand, if a woman really wants a man, nothing will stop her. It's no use being covered in pimples, dressed like a tramp, or smelling like a turnip – nothing puts them off. In desperation you can say, 'I'm ill, I've had chicken pox, you'll catch it. . . . I've terrible diarrhoea. . . . ' It's all in vain. My friend Askew was once pursued by a woman so fiercely he cried, 'I'm impotent. Utterly and helplessly impotent. And homosexual as well. I'm an impotent homosexual. I cannot possibly make love to you.' It was no use, the girl merely said it didn't matter, he hadn't met the right girl yet, her little tricks would cure his impotence, and his homosexuality come to that.

'I may take years before I recover from the experience,' said Askew later. 'Any decent judge would have given her ten years.'

I always feel convention is rather unfair on men in this respect. They need the sort of excuse a woman can use, such as, 'I've got a period,' 'I think I've got a headache coming,' 'I'm suffering from pre-menstrual tension,' and so forth. Askew once tried saying, 'I am suffering from the male menopause,' but all to no avail.

A girlfriend alleges that a good way of deflecting importunate women is to wear braces and a belt. 'No self-respecting girl could make love to a man wearing braces *and* belt,' she said. Perhaps scientists will invent a special grease that can be smeared behind the ears for the purpose of putting off women, although in my own case the difficulty is attracting them.

But to return to the uselessness of trying to bribe women to love you. For years, when I wanted to seduce a girl, I would take her to the best Italian restaurant in London (in Richmond to be precise). It was not cheap. And it was not successful either. Over the years I must have spent thousands of pounds at that restaurant, for a success rate of two feels, a grope, five kisses, ten pecks on the cheek and twenty-four squeezes of the hand. Oh, sorry, I forgot, there were also thirty-five 'Thanks-for-a-lovely-evening-Mike-do-you-mind-if-I-don't-ask-you-in. . . .'

I was a familiar face there. The waiters even got to know me and would try to help. As they came up with the long and expensive menu, they would whisper to the girl, 'Oh, the *signor*, he is a fine man. A big, strong man. Look at those thighs, those shoulders. Undoubtedly the *signor* would make a girl very 'appy indeed. Oh, the *signorina* is a very lucky woman. . . .' Meanwhile, the girl would smile in an embarrassed way and think what a nice man the waiter was – much nicer than Mike, who was obviously half-pissed already, and she would cross her nylon-clad legs even more firmly and think how she could avoid Mike's clawing hands after the meal. Perhaps it would be better to invite him in for coffee and then tell him she thought of him as a friend, one of her greatest friends, and let's not spoil it all. . . .

I don't wish to appear mercenary but I do wish women would make declarations of true friendship *before* they have consumed £25 of food and drink, not after the meal. Askew told me that once, over a first course of smoked salmon at an expensive restaurant, a girl showed him a photograph of her boyfriend, the first time she'd mentioned him. Realizing it was to be a wasted evening, Askew promptly cancelled the rest of the meal and called for the bill. His only concession to gallantry was to ask the girl if she wanted a lift, as he would be going in her direction.

One of the desperations of life for men is that, after they have laid siege to a girl with every device in the rulebook, she takes up with some ugly lout who treats her with contempt and who probably has all the qualities she rejected you for. A girl once told me I was too selfish and too old for her and promptly went out with a man twelve years older than me. I don't know about being selfish, but he was married and refused to see her more than twice a week. To make matters worse she seemed quite happy. I often asked myself: what is this strange power I have over women?

A baffling reason for rejection by a woman is that she is being

treated 'like a sex object'. I often wonder what would happen if
a man said to a girl, 'Of course, you do understand I'm not one
of those filthy beasts who indulge in sex, don't you?' But,
whatever reasons are given, don't believe perseverance will
change a girl. The side of St Pancras station is putty compared
with a woman's mind.

The ultimate way of obtaining a woman's favours is
marriage. Frankly, I feel that is totally immoral. What sort of
man has to tie down a decent girl like that? I think it was in a
Somerset Maugham play that a character says that marriage is
when you want to sleep with a woman so much you offer her free
board and lodging for the rest of her life. No self-respecting
person would stoop to marriage except for money or to have
children.

Offering marriage is as bad as pretending to love a girl to gain
her favours, although that ruse can backfire. I remember my
friend Askew telling me that, years ago, he was so desperate to
make love to an unwilling woman that he said as a last resort,
'But I love you. I love you desperately.'

'That's the whole trouble,' sighed the girl. 'If you didn't
adore me I'd let you make love. But it would hurt you too much
when we had to part. I don't want to break your heart.'

Askew tried to switch tack by immediately bellowing, 'Love
you? Of course I don't love you. I was telling a lie. I detest you
and now let's go upstairs and get cracking.' This too, failed
completely. Strange creatures, women.

But, despite it all, there are still some wheezes and ruses
which Coarse Lovers can use to persuade the opposite sex and
improve their lot. To be in the third team of love does not mean
you never get a game, if I may continue the sporting analogy.

First, remember that women prefer exciting lies to dull facts,
as long as you obey the rules of this tortuous game. Not that
women are alone in this. Truth is the first casualty of any
engagement in the battle of life. To find that out, try buying a
house or selling a car. I never heard of a boss who admitted he
was over-paid or a politician who confessed he was a corrupt
idiot. Love isn't any different from the rest of life. As they used
to say in the army, 'Bullshit baffles brains.'

An excellent way of gaining the interest of women is to feign an unusual condition. This can be physical, mental or even spiritual. The most successful person I ever knew at this was a chap called Charlie in Birmingham some years ago. Charlie had once had an operation for TB in which a small piece of lung had been removed, and at parties he would simply sit by himself with a bottle of Scotch, coughing frequently and paying no attention to anyone. If it was a respectable party, he would arrive early and sit on the piano stool, playing a few idle chords (which were all he knew). He paid no attention to women.

Eventually, feminine curiosity being aroused, some female would come over and ask if he was all right. Charlie would swivel round on the piano stool, look at her with bloodshot eyes, take a large swig of whisky, and reply, 'All right? All right? Of course I'm all right. I can still breathe through the other lung, can't I?'

The girl, all tenderness, would try to investigate this remarkable statement and Charlie would expand his theme by saying, 'Look, sweetie, you're a lovely girl, so don't bother any more with me. Go and get yourself some red-blooded young athlete and stop worrying about a one-lunged cripple like myself. I'll get by. After four years in a sanatorium you. . . .' At this point he would be interrupted by a terrible outburst of coughing and retching.

'But can't they do anything for you?'

'Do? Do?' (a bitter laugh). 'Oh yes, they've done something all right. They've cut a chunk out of one lung, that's what they've done. Isn't modern medicine wonderful?'

'But you've got a dreadful cough.'

'Sorry about that. Some people don't let me go to their parties because I cough so much. One of my so-called friends has got a wife who won't have me round for a meal because she can't stand blood on the tablecloth. I even had to give up playing the piano. The keys got glued up with phlegm.'

'How awful! What sort of person would stop you going to a party just because you cough?'

'The sort of person with a fast sports car, who's successful with women, ducky. Women don't want sick people around.

They want life and the prospect of creating new life, and you can't blame 'em.'

As the party went on you could hear nothing but this terrible booming cough in the corner, and the more Charlie coughed and rasped out his pleas for the girls to go away and not waste their lovely youth on a man with one lung the more the girls adored him. Sometimes, however, as the whisky took over, Charlie would overdo things, and say, 'The irony of it is that the treatment they're giving me actually increases sexual potency. Huh! Fat lot of good that is when you've got five years to live.'

I never found out what happened when Charlie actually got into bed, but his technique appeared astonishingly successful. It was certainly better than mine, which at that youthful period of my life consisted of drinking myself into insensibility and hoping some woman would carry me off. They rarely did.

Of course, the interesting condition need not be merely physical. Charlie hinted at mental and spiritual torment as well. My old friend Watkins (who is a distant cousin of Askew, although less psychopathic) claims he had some success by alleging he had been in a monastery and was under a vow of chastity, which provided women with a challenge they couldn't resist. A mental condition might be simulated – 'I have been working on my thesis about the increase in the numbers of nine-legged spiders for five years, and I'd forgotten what women looked like until I saw you. Tell me, do they still dance backwards?'

I suppose the ultimate challenge is to say firmly, 'I have no sexual feelings at all. No woman has so far been able to arouse me.' After all, we have seen earlier what happened when Askew claimed to be impotent and was dragged to bed.

It need hardly be said that Askew is well versed in these techniques, although he really does go too far. 'I shouldn't be here,' he used to say to a girl in his bachelor days. 'Not with all these women around. The doctor's told me he won't be responsible if I make love. Whatever happens I must not make love until the stitches have healed. *I must not make love tonight.*'

Obviously, this lunatic statement would be found false when they got into bed, but women never seemed to mind the harmless fairy tale. In the great game of love it doesn't matter how you play, as long as you don't break the rules (as by walking up to a girl and asking her to jump into bed).

Some useful statements which will provide a challenge to girls are:

'My first wife was so wonderful nobody could ever take her place.'

'My first wife was so hideous she put me off women for ever.'

'My work at the hospital is so demanding I have to suppress all emotions. You can't operate on a fragilated spindoza when you're thinking of a girl.'

'I've never had any experience of women. There weren't any at the leper colony.'

'A girl once shot herself because I couldn't marry her.'

'A girl once shot *me* because I wouldn't marry her.'

'Ever since a girl left me because I had polio, I have distrusted women.'

'I am training for the Tour de France and the sponsors won't allow me to have sex.'

Many men make the mistake of trying to gain a girl's affections by taking part in her hobbies and interests. Don't. It's a waste of time. First of all you just make yourself thoroughly miserable, as when I came out of a pop concert so deafened I couldn't hear what the girl said when she asked if I'd enjoyed it. It had sounded like someone playing on bedsprings. And, secondly, it won't stop you getting the old heave-ho in the end just the same, if the old heave-ho is on the cards. Besides, should the affair last, the man is condemned to an eternity of visiting places he doesn't like, unless he's the courage to admit he lied in the first place. That's why one often hears women sniping at men ('You always used to be so interested in art and now you shudder when I suggest a visit to the Tate.').

My old pal Watkins once went out with a girl who believed the earth was flat. She was a member of a strange religious sect and poor Watkins used to go with her every Sunday evening to a little hall in Uxbridge and gaze at her lovely figure (which wasn't flat), while everyone sat around telling each other the earth was flat but it didn't matter because the whole lot was going to explode at any moment and everyone was doomed except them.

It started to have an effect on Watkins. When someone asked him to go sailing to France he got quite anxious. 'Are you sure we won't go over the edge?' he asked. Eventually the affair finished but Watkins found the effects lingered for months. The sect kept ringing him up and saying, 'Brother, we haven't seen you at our discussion meetings recently.' Since Watkins didn't like to say the reason was he had stopped sleeping with Sister Maclaren, he found an excuse difficult. In the end the only way he could stop their persecution was by saying he had looked at a map and he now believed the earth was round.

Watkins seems to attract women with strange interests: one of his girlfriends asked him to go sky diving with her. 'I don't know what she wanted' said Watkins. 'Perhaps she was intending to have it off at thirty thousand feet with smoke canisters strapped to our backs. Anyway, I made it clear it was me or sky diving. Never was much good at heights. She chose sky diving.'

A good example of the importance of being firm from the start.

A big difficulty in attracting women is that not only do *you* not know what they want, they don't know themselves. They will tell you they are going out with Fred 'because he's so kind'; next minute they have chucked Fred and are going out with Joe, 'because he's so fascinatingly cruel'. Furthermore, women don't have a great knowledge of how *other* women's minds work. One of the great fallacies of sex is the belief that all women are kin to one another and only women know the mysterious thought processes of each other's minds. That is absolute baloney, as it would be with men.

Women's advice about other women isn't infallible just because it comes from a female. What women say is frequently influenced by their own fantasies. I recall a friend's wife telling me the way to conquer a particular girl was to be romantic and prostrate myself at her feet. Well, I showered her with flowers and chocolates and prostration, and she responded by going out with a man whose idea of affection was to let her clean his car. I used to wonder how the woman could have given this bum advice, until I realized the flowers and the affection were what she herself would have liked and didn't get with four kids and a husband in the rat race.

This doesn't apply only to advice to be kind. Be equally wary of suggestions to 'treat a girl rough. Show her who's boss' and so on. They usually come from women who'd like to be dominated.

My married friend has wrecked the lives of nearly every bachelor in the neighbourhood with her well-meant advice. She is particularly bad at spotting when a girl is sexually inhibited, since she is incurably romantic, and many a young man has wasted weeks of courtship on some iceberg of a female at her behest.

This woman introduced her brother to one of her friends. A sort of affair began but the girl was difficult to pin down and he got the usual advice about flowers and romance. This had no effect so after three weeks, he tried his own course. He rang the girl and said, 'You are right. We are seeing too much of each other. I don't think we should meet tonight.'

She insisted on keeping the date. When they got home he said he wouldn't come in for coffee and was dragged in. He avoided the sofa so she sat on the arm of his chair. At midnight he said he really ought to be going and thirty seconds later he found himself in bed with the girl. His last effort was to say, 'We really shouldn't be doing this,' but she stopped the sentence in midstream by biting his left thigh.

'It was one of the happiest affairs I ever had,' he told me later, limping slightly. 'Every time it went wrong I just vanished for a few days and it all came right again.'

So much for women's instincts about other women. Men's advice is no better. They, too, tend to indulge their own fantasies, knowing they won't have to carry them out. Don't take any notice of saloon-bar rubbish like, 'Why don't you put her over your knee and spank her. . . ? I wouldn't put up with a girl who treated me like that, I'd show her who was boss. . . .' etc. Sex is the greatest spectator sport in the world, and everyone thinks they know better than the poor sucker down on the field.

4 *Starting an Affair*

Is that a six gun in your pocket or are you just pleased to see me? MAE WEST

Making love to a computer — terrible mistake at the singles bar —
Unpleasant incident at publishing party — importance of first date —
Unpleasantness at tennis club — what won't attract women — no use
exposing yourself — how Askew lost the love of his life

What sort of woman should a man choose? I shouldn't worry about it. This is usually decided by accident, such as who stands next to you at the bus stop, or by the woman. Men have no say in the matter at all. However, there are certain types of women to avoid at all costs. They include food-cranks, weirdies, trend-setters, women who talk while making love, and girls who are always late ('That includes most of them,' says Uncle Walter cynically).

A ready-made source of eligible females can be provided by a friendship or dating agency, or through advertisements in magazines. At least, that is the theory but it isn't so simple as it appears. To start with, any woman who has to apply to a computer to get a boyfriend may not be very attractive or may have something wrong with her. In the same way, any man who is reduced to advertising to get a woman may have something wrong with *him*. Sometimes the trouble can be revealed by the advertisements themselves:

Divorced man, 57, fed up with women who will not pull their weight about the house, is seeking good-looking girl, about 23, good cook, clean habits, uninhibited, interested in golf, stock exchange, pot-holing and real beer. Send photo and stamped, addressed envelope if return is desired. Gold-diggers need not apply.

One can tell a lot from the women's adverts, too. Avoid those which specify an avoidance of sex either directly or by hinting. Danger signs are phrases such as, 'Widow, 35, tired of men who want only one thing, seeks true friendship. . . .'

The seeker may well find the true friendship finishes at the bedroom door with a cry of, 'That's all you men want! I had enough trouble with my husband over That Sort of Thing. I thought you were different.'

Seemingly quite innocent ads can turn out to be total misrepresentations. A friend who answered one saying, 'Fun-loving divorcee seeks companionship,' found the door answered by what appeared to be an elderly crone and, on inquiring if her daughter was in, was told there was no daughter but if he was the gentleman from the advert please come inside. He sat on the end of the sofa for half an hour drinking endless cups of tea and waiting for a chance to escape.

I must confess to having tried a computer dating agency myself once. Just for an experiment, of course. I mean, surely no one would suggest I can't attract all the women I want, ho, ho, ho. Well, I don't know if I filled the form in wrongly, but it wasn't a success. I asked for a girl who liked older men, who was interested in the theatre and literature and was sexually experienced, and duly arranged to meet my first choice in a pub near Notting Hill Gate.

She said she didn't drink, which I thought a bit odd, as on the computer form I had specified that I did. However, I bought her a lemonade and asked pleasantly, 'Seen any good plays recently?'

'No,' she replied. 'I hate the theatre. I hardly ever go there.'

At this point I began to realize that even computers aren't perfect, but I struggled on and asked why she didn't go to the theatre.

'I don't like it,' she declared firmly. 'It's all that sex. I went to a play once and there was a scene where this young girl took all her clothes off and a man did the same and they did things to each other. I forget what the play was called. Something about horses I think. I shan't go again.'

I desperately tried all points of possible mental contact, but on books too she had the same obsession. 'I like a good book,' she said, 'but not those dirty ones. Did you ever read *Lucky Jim*? I thought it was disgusting.'

So much for the girl who loved the theatre and was sexually experienced. Was it a computer error and had she asked for a twenty-three-year-old lad interested in table tennis and spiritual affairs? Or is there just a chance she didn't like the look of *me*? Or is the whole system no good anyway? We shall never know. At any rate, she said she had to go after finishing her lemonade.

Of my other two choices (the computer allowed three), one stood me up and the other actually brought her boyfriend. She said, 'We'd quarrelled when I wrote to the agency but we've made it up now and he was curious to see what sort of men were so sex-starved they had to go to an agency.' Strangely enough it was a very pleasant evening. We drank enormous quantities of beer in the pub and left vowing eternal friendship all round. The only fly in the ointment was that I still didn't have a girl.

My friend Askew claims that, after a similar unsatisfactory experience, he wrote to the agency and complained:

Dear Sir,

I wish to protest about your service. After paying you £20 for an introduction to a young lady she refused to have sexual intercourse with me. I insist you return the money immediately or else supply sexual intercourse.

A similar service to dating agencies is provided by 'singles' groups and clubs. 'Singles' bars are popular in the USA, but, once again, it isn't all plain sailing. I remember going into a singles bar in New York where I sat down opposite a rather attractive girl of about twenty-eight and we soon got into conversation. Now I reasoned that people wouldn't go into a singles bar unless they wanted companionship with someone of the opposite sex so I chatted away merrily and in five minutes I was quite hooked on the girl. She told me her life story, how she had married and it had all broken up and how she'd been lonely ever since, and I could hardly control myself. Fate had for once intervened on my side. I asked why she left her husband and she replied, 'He got fresh with me.'

'Fresh? How?'

'He wanted me to do things to him. . . .'

'Oh my God, how awful. What sort of things?'

'Intimate things.'

'The rotten swine. Tell me about them.'

'I couldn't even begin to describe them . . . things I had only heard about. . . .'

I panted slightly.

'The unmentionable cad. Why don't you just give me an idea of what he wanted? Then I'll know how vile he was.'

She looked at me in a peculiar way.

'Say, what are you? Some kind of psycho or something?'

I hastily wiped away the saliva and pulled myself together. 'Of course not. I just couldn't believe a man could be so unspeakably hideous. . . . How low can a person get?'

She softened at this.

'No, I guess I did you wrong. I like you. I can see you're not one of those guys who's just after a cheap lay. You're like me. You'd have to know someone for a long time before you had sex with them.'

At this I realized once again that Green's Luck Was Out. Not having the nerve to leave her, I bought drink after drink and listened to stories about her dismal married life until I could decently make an excuse to go.

It will help to save wasted time in attracting women if one is aware of certain phrases they use which will reveal disappointment to come. One is already quoted in the conversation above ('I'd have to know someone for a long time before I had sex with them.'). In fact, the long time usually recedes into eternity. Here are some more danger signals to the Coarse Lover:

'I couldn't make love to a man who wasn't completely crazy about me. . . .'

'I couldn't make love to a married man.'

'Take your hand away.'

'I need time to make up my mind. . . .'

'I don't think sex is important.'

'I couldn't make love to someone who thought I'd go to bed

with him just because he'd taken me out to the theatre and then treated me to dinner. I'd feel so *cheap*.'

'For the last time – *take your hand away*!'

'The man I want would have to have a £200 suit, an important job and an Aston Martin. . . .' (Usually said to some impoverished fellow worker in the lunch break.)

I stress the importance of listening carefully for conversational hints because it is so difficult to tell from outward appearance or indeed from anything else how a girl is going to behave. I had an unfortunate experience over this at a publisher's party once – a book-launching affair – where I was introduced to a tall, fine-looking girl of about thirty who'd recently written a rather sensational book. We talked about it and she gave me an advance copy there and then (authors do that, poor creatures) and I opened it at the first page and read this:

He lay back on the bed with his vast dick steaming . . . she gazed at it in awe mixed with fascination. . . .

Well, I ask you, what would you do? It seemed to me quite plain that this girl not only knew all about it, but wanted to know even more, and, when she began to say how much she enjoyed my books and how I looked younger than she thought I would be, it all seemed so simple. I reasoned that a girl who wrote about steaming dicks wouldn't beat about the bush, so I took her hand, squeezed it, and whispered in her ear, 'How about coming back to my place and looking at my steaming dick?'

I thought this was rather witty actually, but the response was alarming. She clouted me across the face with all her force, knocking the gin and tonic from my nerveless fingers, as they say in the novels. 'You male pig,' she snarled. 'You revolt me. You *and* your dick.'

(In passing I would just like to know who was the clown who invented that idea that women say no when they mean yes? Here was the perfect example of a woman who not only said no, but meant it. I did not press the matter but walked away and vented my feelings by abusing an elderly publisher.)

It is possible all might have been well if I had not committed the fatal error of speaking bluntly. I have already said that truth flies out when love flies in. I think it was Askew who once asked a girl out and, thinking to put the relationship on an honest basis from the start, said, 'I'll probably be a bit pissed after the meal and try to grope you, but I expect you're used to that.' The girl stood him up and wrote that she despised him.

Be careful if conducting an affair at work. Romances between the lower orders – clerks, typists, messengers and so forth – can be conducted freely, rather in the way slaves were encouraged to breed on the old Southern US plantations. But among higher ranks there is a stern pecking order. Never seduce the secretary of someone higher than yourself, unless you wish to end your business career abruptly. Or unless you can keep it secret. The worst of it is that business bosses are so megalomaniac that they fancy all sorts of women all over the office and regard them as private property. An innocent flirtation with the tea lady may arouse the wrath of some senior executive who has secretly fancied her for years. Thus all affairs should be kept as furtive as possible. If you can, try to find out the preferences of senior staff to avoid making blunders.

Don't hesitate to use your own position (if any). Remember that if young Stiggins wishes to get a good report he'd better stop asking your secretary out for a drink.

The first date with a girl is extremely important, for if things go wrong the first date can easily be the last. Unfortunately, the first outing isn't usually the best. When two comparative strangers go out together the evening is frequently marked by long, strained silences and polite remarks. I firmly believe the first date should be with other people to break the ice. (I'm only referring to the first part of the evening, of course. I'm not suggesting an audience when you're grappling on the sofa.) I don't believe one can beat the wheeze of having a meal and inviting another couple or two. These guests will be under strict instructions not to say anything truthful about you. The task of the females will be to arouse your partner's curiosity by referring to your charm with women, coupled with the challenge that no one can catch you. The man's job is to wait for a suitable moment to whisper, 'I shouldn't say this, but Mike is perhaps the most generous man I know a very brave man/ perhaps the most well-balanced person I've met/ a man who desperately needs a woman to look after him/ the most popular person in Western Europe,' according to the girl's character and tastes.

It is advisable to discuss with your friends beforehand what they are to say. Once, in a foursome at a restaurant, a friend took advantage of my absence for a moment to tell a girl how gentle I was. Five minutes later, under the impression I was expected to be strong and bold, I had a terrible row with the waiter. I thought I was being commanding and masculine but was, according to the girl 'a filthy-tempered racist' (well, I did call him an Italian idiot but only after he said Englishmen knew nothing about wine).

Make sure your friends can be trusted. Do not invite people who will say things like, 'You're not his usual type, he normally goes for blondes,' or 'Did he ever tell you about the time he took out a sixteen-year-old girl?' Later they will apologize ('I'm sorry, old chap, I thought she knew all about your wife,') and it will be too late.

Under no circumstances take a girl to a party for the first date. I speak with feeling after an unpleasantness at Chobham in Surrey some years back, when I took a girl to a party and she vanished with someone else.

I remember searching the house and the garden in the pitiful belief that she was asleep in some remote corner or else locked in a lavatory, until the truth dawned. And if you *do* take a girl to a party, and she *does* vanish, don't believe her explanation, especially if she returns with a satisfied smile on her face.

One of the biggest hindrances to success in acquiring girls is a car. That seems an absurd statement but so many girls have their own transport that offering a lift home can be useless. Better to be offered a lift. I once spent an evening sitting with a pretty new girl at the tennis club and I could see no way of pressing my suit that night, since she had a car, when another man (the swine) leaned forward and said to the girl, 'Will you give me a lift home?' This was a hunnish trick, because his car was actually standing outside the clubhouse, but the ruse worked – she said yes, and they left together. Years later I used the same wheeze myself with equal success. Only this time I asked the girl to drive me back to the club to fetch my car in the morning. 'I thought you didn't have one,' she said severely and I had to confess. She didn't appear to find it as funny as I did.

Incidentally there is no need to be jealous of the man with the enormous sports car and the pretty girl beside him. Many men use a fast car as compensation for their own sexual inadequacy. I find the same tends to apply to women. The girl with the fast car is so often inadequate in some way. My definition of inadequate, of course, is someone who makes me feel inadequate or who's got more money than me. Even so, experience teaches that the most suitable girls drive small cars, 900 c.c. Fiats or old Morris Minors.

Women are not normally impressed by vulgar physical displays. At least that's what is usually believed, although I'm not so sure when I see their lustful little eyes gleaming at some blond hulk of a man. In his youth Askew was known to greet a girl on their first date with lunatic references to his physique such as, 'Sorry I'm late. I'm afraid my trousers burst. I'm so generously endowed. It's happened before. They don't make trousers like they used to. Now where shall we go?' By this time the girl was usually backing away in alarm as Askew, his face suffused with animal desire, patted her buttocks paternally, and then took her arm.

In the matter of bodily display, however, convention's rather hard on men. Women can dress as seductively as they like, with bosoms hanging out of dresses even on formal occasions, but men can't. If a man tried to go into a smart restaurant wearing a kilt as brief as a mini-skirt he'd be thrown out. I sometimes feel we are a little tough on those pathetic male flashers who keep getting arrested in Hyde Park, when females are allowed to flash legally.

A great sexual fallacy is that success in life automatically attracts women. This is not so. It's the appearance of success that draws them – the large car, the smart suit, the subservient underlings – but almost any sales manager can manage this. However, some of the most successful people don't look like successes. I remember watching a girl talking to a famous playwright, whom she later described as 'that horrible little man covered in dandruff'. When I told her who he was she said, 'Why didn't you say so before? He asked me to go out with him and I was rude. How was I to know he was really so attractive?' There are times when I find it difficult to understand women.

The only time 'success' has helped me was when I wrote an article for a Fleet Street newspaper which printed my photograph beside it, and I received a letter from a girl which can only be described as extremely passionate. Unfortunately, she gave no address. A week later I got an even more passionate letter, this time describing in some detail what she would like me to do to her. Still no address. I became desperate with frustration. We began to insert appeals on the sports page:

Would the girl who wrote to Michael Green about his recent article on foul play in British rugby and signed herself Stephanie, please send her address as she has won the prize for the best letter of the week.

This produced a third letter, even more passionate, but no address, and we gave up.

It would take a bold man to say what women want from a man since they don't appear to know themselves. But they do like a man to appear interested (I think). This is in the widest sense. Ignoring a girl is a form of interest; so is beating her up. ('Loves yer? Of course I loves yer. Knocks yer abart, don't I?' as the Cockneys used to say.) The one thing they can't stand is not being needed. Besides, women go for what they *think* is a man's character. This frequently bears no relation whatsoever to the real person and I write as one who has just heard a loud-mouthed braggart described by a girl as 'a terribly genuine person'. If a girl wants a man to be cruel, she'll manage to read cruelty into the simplest actions. I once went out with a girl who had a desperate desire to be dominated. Since I wasn't very dominant, she invented a new personality for me. 'One lump of sugar or two, dear?' I would ask and she'd shriek, 'That's right, trample all over me. You know you'll just shove in as much sugar as you want without bothering about me, so why ask, you beast?'

On the other hand, a girl will manage to read tenderness into the vilest actions of a man if she wants to. One girl, whose husband beat her up, told me when she recovered, 'He may be a little thoughtless at times but he can be very tender, too. After breaking my nose last week he insisted on driving me to hospital.'

But it is useless to act out of character to impress a woman. The true strain always shows through in the end. I always think of my pal Ginger in the army, who told his girl, 'I'm pretty handy with my fists, you know,' and she said, 'Good. I want you to tackle a man who's just insulted me.' Ginger's reply – 'I will if he's smaller than me' – didn't do him much good.

Ginger should have used one of Askew's little wheezes. In his youth, if he took a girl to a party, he would arrange beforehand with some friend to upset wine or beer all over the girl. Askew would then say quietly, 'Leave this to me, my dear. If you are squeamish I should move away as the sight of a man being beaten to a pulp is not very pleasant.' He would then take the man to task and he would play his part by pretending to be terrified of Askew and apologizing deeply.

But as a general rule never get involved in defending a woman's honour. It may be coincidence, but whenever a woman complains someone has been rude to her it's always the toughest man in the room, never somebody you could deal with. Given a choice between being beaten up or losing the woman, a man of honour has no option but to lose the woman. You owe it to yourself.

So great is the competition for girls today (there are now more men than women in the population) that no one can afford to pass up a chance. If any of these wheezes produces success don't let the opportunity slip. My own greatest mistake in this respect came after the tennis club dance. It was pitch black as I lurched into the car park, when suddenly a female crushed up against me and kissed me passionately.

'I've always had a thing about you, Mike,' she whispered. I drunkenly clawed at her, but she pressed her fingers to my lips and said, 'Not now. I've got my husband waiting. Later. I adore you, Mike dear.' With which she slipped swiftly away. It was only after she'd gone I realized I didn't know who she was. I'd forgotten to ask her name and I certainly didn't recognize her immediately. But I thought I knew and when next evening I saw her alone in the club bar I was sure. I walked up to her, placed my arm firmly round her pretty waist and stuck my tongue in her left ear.

'Hi, good-looking,' I said cheerfully.

The rotten bitch trod on my feet with all her force.

'When I want someone as repulsive as you sticking their tongue in my ear I'll let you know, Michael Green!' she bellowed. 'Whatever made you suddenly start that sort of thing with me?'

I was about to reply, 'What you said last night,' when I realized what had happened. It was the wrong girl. I have spent all my time ever since looking for the one who kissed me in the car park but she has never revealed herself and I can't recognize her. I certainly can't go round cross-examining every woman in the tennis club ('Are you the girl who kissed me in the car park after the dance?'). So, if Fate is kind, for heaven's sake get her name and phone number.

In his single days, Askew had a similar experience, but even worse. He met a girl at a party and during a night of passion she wrote her phone number in red biro on his buttocks. In the morning he absentmindedly had a bath and then twisted desperately in front of the mirror only to find by now most of the number had been washed away. He even rang me up and asked me round to see if I could make out the missing digits while he bent over, an unpleasant and futile task.

'I would have married her,' says Askew bitterly. 'Any woman with the imagination to write her telephone number on your arse must be quite a girl.'

To make matters worse, Askew had been drinking so heavily he couldn't really remember what the girl looked like. The chief clue to her identity was a varicose vein on her left leg. For years after that Askew went around peering at women's calves. Sometimes they became rather annoyed.

If you do make a mistake like that, invent a few lies to comfort yourself, such as, 'She would have been all right for a short time but she would have been hell to live with.' Just keep repeating that and drinking a glass of Scotch every time. In about half an hour you'll wonder what you ever saw in the woman.

In the end, though, the whole affair of attracting a woman seems to boil down to some sort of instant chemistry. You can try all the wheezes in the book and fail. Then one golden day you meet someone and talk for an hour and there is nothing need be said except, 'Your place or mine?'

PS Askew says there *is* something more to be said. Never go to their place. You're sure to find the builders are at work or their flatmate has arrived home unexpectedly and the chance is lost and may never return again.

5 *Making Love*

Is sex dirty? Yes, if you do it properly.   WOODY ALLEN

Making the first move – the long, long crawl across the carpet – 'Lie down and have a cup of coffee' – the car test and other lies – beware of stimulants – Askew's revolting meal – sex for the crippled

The title of this section is perhaps rather misleading. I do not intend to explain the mechanics of sex, since if the reader doesn't know them by now he's wasting his time reading this book, but I do intend to give some helpful wheezes on the act of making love which may help a Coarse Lover avoid some of the disasters to which he is natural prey.

The act of lovemaking itself, with its undignified positions and strange noises, is a rather bizarre affair I always think, and I feel some sympathy with medieval philosophers who concluded that God must have ordained it this way deliberately as a joke, to show us how unimportant is puny man and how ridiculous his begetting. But, however strange the contortions of lovemaking, they are as nothing compared with the contortions a man frequently goes through *before* making love.

Let me explain. One of the biggest difficulties in making love to a girl is the first pass. Many acts of love begin with an invitation to 'come in for coffee', after which the unhappy male finds himself seated on a chair six feet from his partner, holding a cup of coffee which he doesn't want, and desperately trying to think of some way of making the first physical contact.

I often wonder if girls appreciate the sheer physical humiliation which the man undergoes on these occasions. What happens is that the man finds some sort of excuse for getting on the floor (like dropping a spoon) and then crawls to the girl's chair on hands and knees, kneels up and tries to peck the face of his beloved. This isn't too bad if the results are successful and both start to grapple but, if rebuffed, the poor man has to crawl back to his own chair like a beaten dog, after which there is one of those terrible silences broken only by desultory remarks in which both parties are frightfully polite to each other.

So it is worth exploring alternatives to crawling across the carpet. One is to go to the toilet and on return lean over the back of the girl's chair and slobber all over her hair. That is assuming she has the sense to stay there and not take out the coffee cups as you return. Another alternative is to grab the girl round the waist as she stands at the stove making coffee. Then there is a wheeze recommended by my old Uncle Walter, in which the man cries from upstairs, 'I cannot flush the toilet.' The girl will come up and deal with the emergency and that will break up the hypnotic impasse downstairs. In theory one should just walk up and kiss her, but a surprisingly large number of men get afflicted by Coarse Lover's Paralysis and find themselves totally unable to make the first move.

A girlfriend told me a dental student made the initial opening by asking to see her teeth.

'I watched when you smiled just then,' he said, 'and I'll bet a hundred pounds those fillings were done by someone trained at Guy's Hospital. You can always tell a Guy's filling. Sometimes you can even identify the man who did it. Now open your mouth and let me see if I can tell who did those. . . .'

As the girl said, 'Never open your mouth for a dental student.'

If the response to any of these moves is, 'Please don't do that,' leave as soon as possible. Don't bother to ask why you are being rebuffed. You won't receive the real reason, which is perhaps just as well, as it may be that you are totally repulsive. Standard replies are, 'I don't know why, I seem to have gone off sex recently,' 'I'm heavily involved with a terribly nice man,' 'I've never thought of you in that way.' Any attempt to piece together logic from these will drive you bonkers, especially as two days later the girl who has 'gone off sex recently' will be seen hanging for dear life on to some man's arm and rubbing her lovely breast on his elbow. Not that I blame the girls. As I've said before, don't expect different standards in sex from everyday affairs. Humans don't like to hurt people by telling the truth.

After the rebuff the man looks at his watch and says, 'Goodness, I didn't realize it was so late. I have to be in Birmingham by ten o'clock tomorrow (in Sheffield at nine, at work by eight).' And the girl must reply, 'Are you sure you won't have another cup of coffee?' (putting away the coffee as she says so) and the man says, 'No, I must go, thanks so much for inviting me in.' The girl replies, 'No, thank *you* for a lovely evening,' and the man leaves as rapidly as possible, giving a phoney wave and smile as she shuts the door, after which both breathe a sigh of relief.

Society desperately needs an acceptable phrase as a substitute for 'coffee' to avoid all this rubbish. How about: 'Would you like a stick of peppermint rock?' Then the man or woman merely has to say yes or no and other variations such as, 'I don't feel like peppermint rock tonight, but I'd like some another time.' It would be my luck to say yes and be served with a bowl of peppermint rock.

As an example of how absurd the convention has become, I should like to tell what happened when I met a lovely girl at a party. It was an instant and mutual attraction. Our eyes met and flashed the unspoken message. Later I offered her a lift home. As we got into the car I said, 'Would you like to come back to my place for a cup of coffee?' She replied without any hesitation, 'Yes, I would love to, but I must warn you I have no contraception.'

That was the start of a lovely relationship which only ended when she went abroad. It is ridiculous, though, that women are now reduced to saying, 'Yes, I'd like a cup of coffee, but just a cup of *coffee* if you don't mind, as I have to get up early.'

Yet frankness is not necessarily the answer. Even the most liberated girls prefer sexual invitations wrapped up in pink paper, so to speak. I doubt if anyone will achieve much success by saying to a girl, 'Would you like to come in for a grope?' the first time she is taken out. (NB Since writing that paragraph I have tested the idea. No, it doesn't work.)

A useful guide as to whether there is any chance of success is the car test. When driving a girl home, say on arrival, 'Is it all right to park here?' If she says, 'It doesn't matter for a short time,' don't even bother to go indoors. If she says, 'Well, the police do sometimes tow cars away after they've been here two or three hours,' rush inside (after first moving the car round the corner).

I am indebted to my old friend Mr Geoff Webb of Ealing (who was featured in *The Art of Coarse Drinking* for collapsing drunk in a university mile race) for an interesting variation. When he was at an American university in the sixties, contraceptives used to be obtained for half a dollar from a machine in the men's room of the local garage. While driving a girl home it was a good idea to stop at the garage, ask the attendant for two 50 cent pieces for a dollar, visit the men's room and watch the girl's reaction. If she frowned, the signs were bad. If she smiled, the half-dollar was not going to be wasted.

However, assuming the first moves have been made and the girl is willing, we now come to lovemaking. Resist any temptation to improve this by aphrodisiacs for either party. No normal person is likely to fill himself up with powdered rhino horn, or his partner with Spanish Fly, but it's surprising how many men like to think there's something that does them good sexually, whether it's cocoa, cheese, oysters, stout or even those strengthening tablets they used to sell down the Charing Cross Road under that great sign:

GAUTIER'S CAPSULES
The Great Rejuvenator

Askew once found himself unable to perform sexually, so the next time he took out a girl to dinner he stuffed himself with aphrodisiac foods, starting with oysters and liberally consuming asparagus, celery and spinach with plenty of liver.

'It did nothing for my sexual performance,' he said, 'although it cleared up all my pimples. What happened was that, just as I got into bed with her, I felt violently sick and had to rush to the lavatory. It was some consolation that I had a wonderful erection at the time, but that had vanished by the time I got back and all I wanted to do was sleep.'

Yet Askew has never lost a secret belief that cocoa is the finest stimulant of all. After taking a girl to a smart restaurant for dinner he has been known to order brandy and cocoa. Others swear by liver, or something nauseous such as raw eggs (strange how aphrodisiacs, like hangover cures, are often sick-making). A nurse I used to know was in the habit of offering her boyfriend a whiff of oxygen. One of them misunderstood her meaning and was discovered playing a jet of oxygen over his vital parts with a pleased smile on his face. He was rather disappointed to be told he was supposed to sniff it.

I am cynical about the supposed stimulus of cannabis. I have only smoked cannabis once in my life and, instead of turning me on (as I believe they say in the drug scene), it made me intensely irritable. I think it was because I knew it was highly illegal and I was scared of being arrested. A most unsatisfactory night was had by all. I kept waking up every time a car went by and shouting, 'Is it the police?' My partner didn't get a wink of sleep and I left at dawn, convinced we were going to be raided.

Alcohol is well known as the Great Deceiver of Love. As Shakespeare says in *Macbeth*: '. . . it sets a man on and takes him off; it makes him stand to and not stand to.' But the effects are so subtle that, after a couple of drinks, it seems impossible that this kindly, good friend could do anything but stimulate one to hitherto unimagined feats of love. Possibly one is, in fact, better after a couple of drinks. I wouldn't know – I've never been able to stop at a couple. Guinness is traditionally a good sexual stimulant but it has an anti-social effect on the lower bowel. Cider and its French liqueur form Calvados have also been highly recommended, but strong beer can be as good as a contraceptive, producing the dramatically named Brewer's Droop or Barmaid's Wilt.

The idea that a girl will hand over her favours if plied with sufficient drink is one of those old-fashioned and rather nasty fallacies that still hang around. Besides, what sort of despicable rat would ply a girl with drink to seduce her? Most men, actually, but it doesn't work, unfortunately. Contrary to common belief, drink won't make a girl do anything she wasn't prepared to do in the first place, unless she is absolutely blotto, in which case she's more likely to be sick. What drink does do to a girl is to make her more free with the outward trappings of affection – hand squeezing and so forth. Attempts to loosen up a girl with drink usually rebound. I well remember Askew pouring drink by the bucket into a woman at a party in an effort to break her will. But she was impervious to alcohol and the only result was that he drank himself into insensibility. His last words, as he slid to the floor with a whisky in his hand, were, 'Why don't we go back to your place and make passionate love, darling?' The woman looked down at him in disgust and snarled, 'With what?'

Askew claims he found the perfect male aphrodisiac in a bar in Marrakesh, but it came in a plain bottle and he forgot what it was called. He alleges that after five glasses he visited a nearby house of pleasure from which he was ejected for having worn out one of the girls.

The best aphrodisiacs are mental. The sight of a suspender belt is enough to revive the drooping spirits of most males. Jealousy is a good stimulant too. If a woman is reluctant to make love and at the same time starts praising other men, the effect on me is magical. Incredible desire fills my whole being. Unfortunately it is usually wasted, because the woman means what she says and rejects any advance.

So much for stimulants. There are also put-offs. The human body is chief among these. People look different in the nude, and the sight of a flabby heap of flesh covered in boils – formerly hidden discreetly under a smart suit – might damp a woman's ardour. Unless you are the possessor of a good frame, therefore, undress quickly and get into bed first, and then your partner won't have a chance to lie there and wonder whether she really wants to make love to all those pimples. Fortunately, women seem to prefer the male to get into bed ahead of them but, if you can't, undress in the gloom if possible. It may be equally disastrous if the man sees the female undressing, so when in bed do not watch the girl disrobing unless you are certain of her lovely form. Some women sort of fall apart when they take their clothes off and the sight of what appeared to be a shapely bosom falling to the waist of the loved one can be distressing. Keep the eyes shut until she is safely tucked in beside you.

Do not comment on your partner's shape. Remarks such as, 'That's funny, one of your breasts is lower than the other,' will only provoke trouble.

An ex-girlfriend told me that the first time she slept with her future husband she had been undergoing medical treatment which involved marking out areas of her stomach with indelible ink. 'Please tell me dear,' said her husband when they got into bed, 'why it is necessary to have a plan tattooed on you showing the way to it? I am quite capable of finding it myself.'

Care is particularly essential if a man has any physical deficiencies. Do not ask for a glass of water in which to put your false teeth, for instance, or demand a hook to hang up your truss. Deal with things like that in the bathroom.

While a Coarse Lover can cope in this way with physical put-offs he must also prepare for mental ones, such as statements by the girl like: 'You've got to marry me now,' or, 'You must meet my father. He's an all-in wrestler.' It's a good idea to have an answer ready in advance. Probably the best for all occasions is: 'You must meet my wife. She's a lawyer.'

Contraception would appear to be no problem now that so many women are on the pill, but a surprisingly large number are not for one reason or another. So it is worth checking your partner is not relying on you in this respect. Few things equal the horror of making the inquiry afterwards and being told, 'I left it to you.' Thus even today it may be wise for a man to carry a packet of Durex, which should be carefully stowed in a safe place. This will avoid the unpleasantness which occurred to a comrade in the army who called on a girl and, while he was showing her parents a photograph, a packet of contraceptives fell from his wallet on to the carpet. The feeble explanation, 'We have to carry these things, it's an order,' was greeted with considerable cynicism and the father took him aside and told him not to lay evil hands on his daughter. She was all for it when they left the house, but fear proved too strong for him.

If Durex are used, it is worth checking the directions. Askew confessed to me recently that in all his life he had never read the instructions on a packet as, when the time came to open it, his hands were shaking so much with excitement.

'Perhaps I have been putting them on all wrong,' he said with sudden alarm. 'Or do you put them on? Perhaps you're supposed to swallow them.'

The horrors of inadequate contraception are well illustrated by what happened to my old pal Watkins when a girl he had spent the night with said in the morning, 'Why don't you get up and make tea? Have you no consideration for a pregnant woman?'

'How long have you been pregnant?' asked Watkins and she replied bitterly, 'About twenty minutes I should reckon, judging by your idea of contraception.'

While on this subject, a friend has an interesting reflex. He always has a sexual urge when he hears the rustle of a paper bag. He attributes it to a holiday with a girl in his student days, when he kept his contraceptives in a paper bag and would grope for them in the dark watches of the night.

Do not make love if suffering from some temporary physical disability such as a strained back or a broken limb. While there is a sense of achievement in overcoming the disability this is often marred by unhappy consequences. I remember going to have Sunday lunch with a friend in a bachelor pad where everyone had a separate bedroom and shared a communal living room. As the main course arrived, we became aware of a knocking from the room above. This got louder and louder and more and more urgent, so we went upstairs to investigate and found my friend's flatmate, whose leg was in plaster up to his groin, helpless on top of a girl. Owing to the huge plaster on his broken leg, he was unable to roll over and the young lady was beating on the floor for help. He was not amused by a suggestion that we threw a bucket of water over them.

A case was reported recently of a young man who sustained a slipped disc while making love in a car and who became locked in a crouching position. The girl was trapped underneath him and had to attract help by blowing the horn with her foot. And my old Uncle Walter to this day limps because of a back injury sustained, he alleges, by making love 'in the bucket seat of a pre-war MG sports car'. As Walter says, 'Just another wound in the Great War of Love, my boy.'

6 *Getting Down to It*

Oi always makes love to me wife in me boots, 'cos it feels more loike adultery. SUFFOLK FARM WORKER

Don't shoot the bed, it's doing its best — perils of eating during intercourse — conventions of the menage à trois — diary of an affair

Where to make love is sometimes a problem, especially in a liaison between two people which cannot be conducted at either party's home – an office affair for example. Borrowing a room in a friend's house is one solution but make sure the friend isn't someone like Askew, who has been known to stand outside with his ear pressed to the wall giving a running commentary. Using the office is a possibility but the fear of discovery is so great you probably won't be able to consummate the affair. It's not much fun making love on the floor of the mail room, listening for the cleaners. Indeed, I once worked with a chap who was so engrossed making love in the telex room he failed to hear the cleaner come in. She took no notice but merely started work, and the first he knew of her presence was when he became aware of a broom passing in front of his face. 'Don't mind me, love,' she said, a cigarette dangling from her mouth, 'but I'll have to ask you to move when I scrub the floor.'

Sex at work is easier as you get higher up, because there's a private office. It is for this reason that the pictures in this book include higher executives in sexual positions.

The most ingenious solution I heard to this problem was that of a couple who met once a week and used a bathroom in the corridor of a large, old-fashioned hotel. They just walked in. It was free, warm and comfortable, it could be locked without suspicion and nobody used it during the daytime. They could also have a bath.

However, if we assume love will be made in a bedroom, it's worth taking a little trouble to make things as pleasant as possible. There are many traps for the Coarse Lover. Clear away traces of previous affairs, such as rude messages in lipstick on the wall, old articles of feminine underwear, photographs of other girls, and so forth. If you are in the habit of cutting notches in the headboard to indicate scores, disguise them, pretend they were made by a deathwatch beetle or say they were caused by biting the headboard out of frustrated love.

Contrary to conventional advice, do *not* have the bedroom full of soft lights and sweet music, as if ready for a female guest. This suggests you expected the girl to jump into bed with you and she may resent this, even though you were obviously right. Askew is even clumsier. Female guests have been known to find a bedroom carefully prepared with a glass of water on each side of the bed, a piece of mistletoe dangling from the headboard, and a row of contraceptives carefully laid out on the bedside table, together with 'Just the Thought of You' on a cassette player and a copy of the Kama Sutra her side of the bed.

Askew claims that in his salad days he changed the cassette after he got into bed to a cha-cha-cha, and performed to the music. This boast got round to Sheila Askew who commented tartly, 'I should have thought the "Dead March" or the "Unfinished Symphony" would have been more appropriate, or perhaps the "Grasshoppers' Ball".'

It is best for the room to look crumpled and casual, a typical bachelor's bedroom – although dirty underwear should be hidden away (not under the pillow). The disarray will be a challenge to the girl by suggesting you are a confirmed bachelor and will arouse her maternal instincts (if any). If you have been fortunate enough to have had a female guest the night before who tidied the room, it may be necessary to untidy it deliberately.

Make sure the curtains are secure. I shall never forget advancing naked upon an equally unclothed girl with a hideous leer on my face one night, and just as I was about to clutch her willing form I happened to glance at the window and saw the woman next door looking in. I don't know how she felt, but I was shattered. Somehow the night was not a success, and I could never bring myself to attend another meeting of the residents' association.

Make sure the bed itself and the mattress are suitable for the task in hand. If a bed develops a creak, buy a new one. *Creaking beds cannot be cured.* It's no use – as soon as you've fixed one creak, another starts up somewhere else. The thought that a creaking bed is revealing to all the neighbours is not conducive to good lovemaking, especially if you've friends in the flat who comment next morning. I used to live in a bachelor flat with four other blokes. One had a girlfriend and the boys used to make sneering remarks about the bed at breakfast – things like, 'I must say old man, your performance is getting worse. Only once, and that hardly lasted two creaks. . . .' In the end the poor girl refused to come to the flat any more.

A colleague tells me he spent his honeymoon in a guest house in a remote part of North Wales. It was kept by an old crone who provided them with an enormous brass bedstead and a feather mattress. What with the mattress and the bedstead, the marriage threatened to remain unconsummated because, as soon as the bedstead started jangling, the old lady would knock on the wall and shout, 'Now, then, just you stop that at once!' The unhappy couple were reduced to taking long walks into the hills to make love, in the great Welsh tradition.

Check the strength of the bed. While everyone would like to boast that the violence of their lovemaking caused the bed to collapse, it is not always convenient when it does so. I cannot say I have ever caused a bed to give way, but I did fall through a camp bed once and my partner was unfortunate enough to be speared by an open tin of pineapples underneath, which ended the lovemaking immediately, although I had some compensation by being allowed to lick the wounds, since saliva is a natural disinfectant. That's a useful thing to know, incidentally. It has gained me many a good lick.

An Irish chum says that, when he was a student, his frequent lovemaking caused a leg to fall off the divan in a Dublin bedsitter, and he replaced it with a jamjar. 'I now know,' he says, 'that the breaking strain of a jamjar is less than the combined weight of two people making love. The bloody thing exploded and filled the room with broken glass.' Nevertheless, he persevered with jamjars, all of which exploded eventually, with the result that people could recognize his girlfriends instantly by the glass in their hair.

Don't make the mistake of choosing the open air for an early consummation. By the open air I mean camping, yachting, and so forth. It's one of the great fallacies of sex that it's all better out of doors. It isn't, as I've described earlier. Making love in a tent not only involves immense care to avoid knocking the thing down, but every single sound can be plainly heard for five miles around. In addition, in hot weather, making love causes the temperature inside a tent to rise to about 85 degrees fahrenheit, and it stays there for the rest of the night. Not to mention the flies, the mosquitoes and the moths who all come inside to watch you and perhaps join in as well. I remember a friend who foolishly went camping for his honeymoon, and who, while zipping up his sleeping bag with trembling hands after making love, caught his member in the zip, causing an abrupt end to the honeymoon. 'I often wonder what people would say if I told them I returned from honeymoon with my tool in bandages,' he says. 'My wife says they would take it as a tribute to her.'

Yachts are as bad. The girl jumps for joy when she's invited, imagining she and her beloved lying together in a huge bed alone at anchor, when in fact she arrives to find three other people are coming because the man has got cold feet about having a crew of only one girl. If the happy couple have the forward berth there is a little privacy – perhaps as much as one would get having sexual intercourse in Trafalgar Square. By squeezing together on a narrow single bunk they can just make love but only at the cost of arousing the entire crew, who wonder why the boat is swaying so much, and what the hell is going on by the forward hatch. This leads to awkward questions from outside such as, 'Why are you moaning and gasping like that Sheila? Are you all right?'

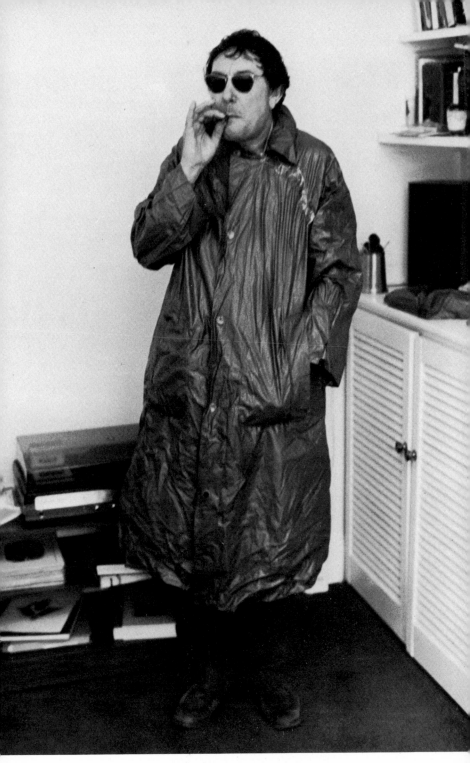

The author welcoming a new female guest to his apartment

Some Interesting Positions

The broom cupboard
Frequently used during office parties

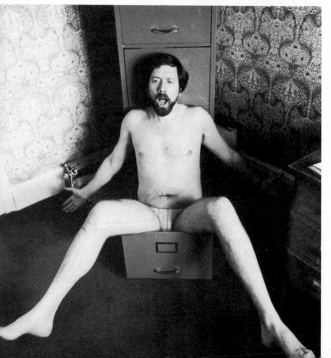

The filing cabinet   Position of male (we tried to show the female, but she quit while we were posing the man). The office boy is not shown (he quit too). The man would have quit but he got stuck in the filing cabinet

The marketing director The surprise element — always possible in office life — is often successful (when not totally disastrous)

he kamikaze (the girl nnot be seen as she is reaming with fear on the or)

Did I hear you correctly?

Never!

Perhaps you'd like a cup of coffee?

Well, it is rather a long way for you to walk home . . . .

But only if we have a meaningful
relationship . . . .

I really don't think we should, first
time out together . . . .

Female Expressions

Yes!

Before we get into bed I must warn
you I may not be much good . . . .

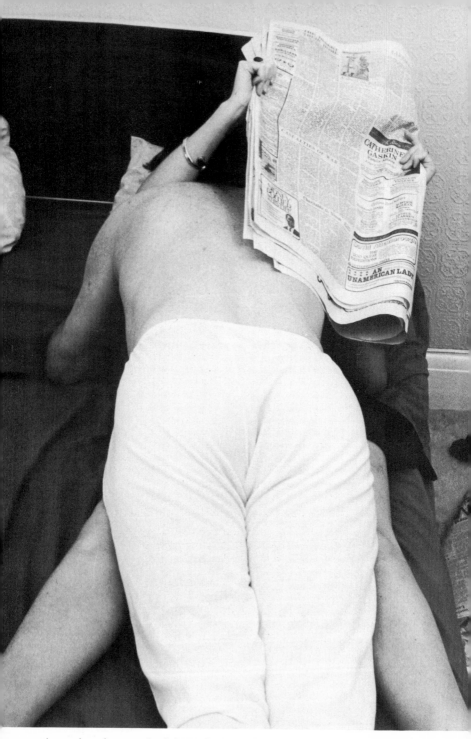

A genuine photograph of the author actually making love. His underwear
has been painted in at the request of the girl's relatives. Shortly after this
picture was taken she fainted

Askew's honeymoon night

Two Approaches to Women
Above:
Australian method of chatting up girl
Below:
European method. The results are the same in each case — someone else gets the girl

In addition, on many small yachts the door to the forward compartment is liable to be opened at any minute, since the same door serves both the toilet and the cabin and if someone closes it on the toilet they must open it on the cabin.

Even when alone on a yacht, the happy pair will find consummation difficult and probably best achieved by fantastic contortions they never realized they were capable of, involving the girl's leg sticking out through a hatch, and so on. All this presumes you aren't too exhausted and ill from a day's sailing to want to make love anyway.

An attempt to make up for the night's frustration by having it off during the day when the others are ashore will inevitably be interrupted by the harbour master or the customs. They have an uncanny instinct for knocking on the cabin roof just as a climax is about to be reached. In any case, the swaying of the masts will have revealed all to everyone for half a mile around.

I'm convinced most of these romantic open-air holidays are totally celibate and the boys and girls have to compensate when they come back. I know when I went camping in Italy with a girl we ended up by hiring a hotel room in which to make love. That was after the Germans in the next tent complained of the noise. 'Vot vos going on last night, hein? We thought it vos the World Cup ha, ha, ha.'

At one point we were driven to going into the deserted hills to find solitude. We did find what seemed an idyllic spot, high up on a plateau but, after we'd made love, we discovered an old Italian shepherd had been looking at us. He said nothing, just shook his head two or three times, and silently padded away.

Who should take the initiative in sex? This is a question often asked and answered in sex journalism. For a Coarse Lover there is only one answer: you. Get It While You Can is the thirty-third Law of Coarse Sex. Hell, you might be asleep in two minutes, or she might change her mind, or you might sober up or get these stabbing pains in the chest again. *Never waste an erection.*

In an effort to improve performance as a lover don't pay too much attention to so-called research into sex and various theories about it, since, as any sociology student will tell you, research into human behaviour can be made to prove anything. A whole industry has grown up around sexual research, with platoons of lovers frantically copulating in laboratories with wires attached to their bodies. Even the rectal temperature is measured. This could account for some of the strange findings, since it must be difficult to make love with a thermometer sticking out of your backside.

When a learned doctor 'discovers' that the knee is the most erogenous zone in 79 per cent of women, it simply means 79 per cent of a small number gave that answer or, more likely, that the doctor researched until he got the answers that fitted his theories. Don't base lovemaking on something read in a book or magazine, or you may spend your life vainly kissing some part of a girl's anatomy which leaves her quite cold. Ask the girl, not the magazine. I write as one who wasted years on slobbering over the back of a girl's ankle, as recommended in some book which described it as a trigger zone. Eventually she said coldly, 'I really don't like saliva all over my ankles if you don't mind.' So much for research.

Uncle Walter has just leaned over my shoulder and said, 'My boy, the one thing that will always stimulate any woman is a well-filled wallet. Your aunt will bear witness to that.' I make no comment.

Do not eat in bed with a partner. Breakfast is particularly vile because of crumbs from the toast or croissant. If you have ever tried to make love in the morning with crumbs all over your loins, you will know what I mean. And so will the girl who, apart from playing hostess to what probably feels like a carpenter's file, may find crumbs creeping in via the bottom sheet. Preserves are even bigger pests than crumbs and can result in foreplay which consists of smearing the girl's nipples with marmalade. In hot climates this could result in a cloud of flies all over her breasts. If that should happen, do not spray insect killer on the affected parts.

Drinking in bed is fine, provided care is exercised. Nothing breaks up a relationship more quickly than spilling hot tea over a nude girl, especially if you later try to make love in the wet sheets. Research by M. Green and others has shown that the male organ does not react favourably to having hot tea spilled over it. As regards alcohol, remember that the mere fact of being in bed with a girl somehow creates a false sense of proportion, and you always pour too much, or go berserk like Askew, who in a moment of romantic delirium anointed his parts with champagne as a libation to Venus. As the wine had been in the ice-bucket, the results were not promising. He recovered after a while, but the girl said afterwards it was like being made love to by a stalactite. If too much drink is taken, both parties may finish up lying side by side, white-faced and breathing heavily, until one rushes for the bathroom.

How much foreplay is used depends on various factors ranging from when her husband will return to what time the last bus leaves. Other limiting factors are the strength of the man's finger and whether the girl responds or continues to look at television. An interesting facet of Coarse Sex is that the foreplay is often carried on in a different room from the actual lovemaking, or even in a different town. Askew, for instance, claims he once began in Luton and consummated the affair in Uxbridge. The foreplay begins downstairs on the carpet or in the car outside and ends with the suggestion, usually made in a panting voice, 'Let's go to the bedroom.' What happens next depends on whether the couple tear off their clothes and jump between the sheets or whether they go through the normal bedtime routine of cleaning teeth, winding watch, saying prayers and so forth. The pattern for this is invariably set by whichever partner is on their home ground. Frequently, foreplay in Coarse Sex ends with the man snoring in bed while the girl, having spent ten minutes in the bathroom, is now saying a Hail Mary before putting out the cat.

It is not always easy to tell if a woman has had an orgasm, especially as they were not invented until 1953, when women's magazines discovered their existence. It is not much use asking her since she won't like to say no, or you might receive the reply I once got: 'Yes, I had one only last week.' The fact that the girl lets out a low moan, followed by a gasp, could well mean she has just remembered she left the electric iron on, rather than that she is fulfilled. If she bites a chunk out of the man's ear it could be a hint she is dissatisfied. However, if there is a sudden screech, followed by the sound of her contact lenses hitting the ceiling it could be taken as indicating the lady is not displeased.

As a general rule, it could also be said that orgasm has not been achieved if the woman (a) continues to talk about the difficulty of getting the phone repaired or (b) wants it again after thirty seconds. If, as a man, you don't know when *you* have had an orgasm, you are beyond human aid.

The period after lovemaking is over reveals yet another clash between the sexes. There is only one thing a red-blooded male wants to do after making love and that is to roll over and go to sleep as quickly as possible. Unfortunately, women don't. The only thing they want to do is talk and they won't rest until they get a reply. They would like to exchange tender endearments and it can be rather hurtful if the man's endearment consists of, 'For heaven's sake unwind your legs from behind my neck, they're killing me.' In fairness to the woman, the man must resist the temptation either to sleep or to get straight out of bed, say, 'Thank you very much, my dear, that was lovely,' put on his hat and leave the house (unless he hears the husband putting the key in the front door). If you must fall asleep, have the courtesy not to do so on top of the young lady. If you light a cigarette, do not lie on top of her blowing smoke into her face or use her navel as an ashtray. This is not the moment to discuss repayment of the money you lent her on holiday. NB Do not make a pencil tick on the wall to indicate another success. Have the courtesy to wait until the girl has left. Do not do as Askew does and start writing notes in a little bedside book, cackling all the time.

It is the height of bad manners to ask the girl if she would mind signing her panties and leaving them behind, especially if you then pin them to the bedroom wall. However, if she should ask *you* to sign them, do so by all means. You are a lucky man, *signor*. . . .

After making love, move into a comfortable position to one side of the girl, keeping one hand in some sort of contact with her – put your thumb in her armpit, for example, but not in such an intimate position as to hint at further lovemaking. With eyes closed let her torrent of prattling sweep over you. Pretend it's water going down the drain. Say 'darling' at intervals of five seconds. If it is all too much, mutter, 'I think I shall be able to manage it again in about half an hour if I have a little doze now.' The effect is magical. With the promise of their favourite activity being repeated, women will instantly shut up. The only trouble is they never forget, and after thirty minutes to the dot you will be woken up to fulfil the pledge. So do not use this defence lightly.

If you are having a relationship with a married woman, there are certain conventions to be observed. This type of affair falls under four headings: 1 When the husband doesn't know. 2 When the husband does know. 3 When the husband does know but won't admit it to himself. 4 When the husband doesn't want to know anyway. It is in the last three that rules must be observed to avoid upsetting the delicate balance of the relationship.

Lovemaking must not be ostentatious. It will only cause trouble if the husband comes home to find his wife and her lover at it hammer-and-tongs as he enters the front door. He must not find the marital bed looking as if a couple of sexual maniacs have been having a festival in it, with his own dressing gown. still warm, lying across the wreckage and his wife's panties glaring at him from the floor. The lover and the wife should not show affection in public, such as groping each other under the table at dinner parties or vanishing into the bushes for half an hour at a barbecue. This sort of thing makes it impossible for the husband to deceive himself, however hard he tries.

The lover must be willing to become a friend of the husband and the family as a whole. Ideally, they should all play bridge together. The usual convention is for the lover to be invited to dinner, perhaps with a girlfriend, and then given a ritual inspection by the husband. If the husband approves, the lover's relationship with the wife will be much better. The husband's ego must be flattered continually. The wife should encourage a feeling of virility by praising his lovemaking, golf, tennis, courage, business record and so on. So should the lover. Askew, when having an affair with a married woman, used to defend her husband with astonishing vehemence.

'I tell you he is one of the whitest men I know,' he shouted at some critics of the man. 'And I ought to know, because I'm sleeping with his wife.'

A further convention the Coarse Lover must observe is that the husband is entitled to know when he has called. This is not stated outright, of course. The wife merely says something like, 'Oh, by the way just after you left this morning Fred looked in for a cup of coffee. He sent his regards and said would you meet him for a drink at the club tomorrow?' These innocent words disguise the truth, which is that Fred burst into the house as soon as the husband turned the corner of the road, grabbed the wife by the buttocks and said, 'Come on, how about having it off straight away?' – a request which was enthusiastically granted. But all three people concerned know this and, as long as the social decencies of adultery are observed, no harm is done.

Children can prove a fly in the ointment. They are not impressed by the social conventions just described, any more than the family dog will be. *They know.* It is no use giving them sweets, or the dog bones, they look at you with an evil glare. The children's reaction is not one of horror, however. They just object to being left out. They know mummy is doing something interesting and they haven't been invited to join in. The dog feels the same way, too. So take them both out for a walk occasionally.

Constant vigilance is needed to keep these rules, and the penalties for infraction are high. As an awful warning of what can happen, let me quote the experience of a Fleet Street friend who unwisely went to dinner at a friend's house after a Press Club reception. He rang me next morning: 'You know what happened after I left the Press Club?'

'No.'

'Exactly. Neither do I. The next thing I remember is waking up in bed at four o'clock in the morning with my dinner-party hostess. I was aroused by her husband coming up to bed.'

'What did he do?'

'Nothing. He just nodded at me and got into bed, so I got out, dressed and went home, where I found my wife had locked me out of the house. I am phoning from a transport cafe. Do you know the number of a good florist? I intend to send flowers to all concerned.'

He sprayed the whole district with flowers for weeks after that, but the memories lingered on. There is always a penalty to be paid for breaking the unwritten code of the eternal triangle.

APPENDIX

The Price of Love (1)   COST

1 June: You go to a party at a friend's place in Chiswick and you meet this interesting girl who is rather pretty and who works quite near your office in the West End. And she is generous and kind and offers you wine when you've drunk your bottle. You ask if you can give her a lift home but she has promised to go home with Daphne her flatmate who doesn't know the way, and you say you will give her a ring next week and she says, yes, that would be nice   Nil

4 June: You did ring and you meet for beer and sandwiches at a pub near her office. And you get on fine and you ask her to the theatre   Beer and food: £3.60

11 June: Take her to theatre. She clutches your arm affectionately. Unfortunately that is all the affection you do get as she lives in Earls Court and you live in Notting Hill Gate. But she squeezes your hand as you say goodbye on the platform   Theatre:£7.50 Drinks: £3.45

14 June: Meet for lunch   Beer and food: £3.60

16 June: This is it. Dinner! You bring the car to the office so you can return to her

flat after the meal. You tell your flatmates
you probably won't be coming back tonight. Unfortunately she has failed to
mention that an old school chum is visiting and sharing her bedroom. So you
come in and make polite conversation
while desire tears at your loins and you
can hardly keep your hands off her. However, she hints it will be all right next time.
Return home to find bedroom occupied by
drunk guest who passed out ('Well, you
said you weren't coming back tonight.')

Parking fines:£10
Dinner: £19.60
Drinks: £4.10
Petrol: £2.50

21 June: This is the next time and it's a
Friday. Extra large and luxurious dinner
in Soho. You drink too much. Car to Earls
Court. The whole flat is empty. Even her
flatmate is away. Seized by passion you try
to make love on the kitchen floor and fail,
perhaps because the milk saucepan boils
over at the moment of attempted insertion. To bed, but even an heroic attack of
fellatio by the girl cannot rouse you. Then,
as dawn creeps through the curtains, you
are woken by something licking your ear
and this time it is all right

Parking fines: £10
Dinner: £23.97
Drinks: £3.60
Scratch on car
caused by pulling
out while cares-
sing girl's thigh:
£15

22 June: Lovely, lazy Saturday morning in
bed making love occasionally. Get up
midday to go to pub with beloved and find
car has been towed away by police. Spend
afternoon at the car pound. But the girl
says, 'I'll treat *you* to dinner tonight at
home,' and makes spaghetti bolognese. As
her idea of wine is half a bottle of red ink
you provide some more (two bottles)

Car penalty: £25
Wine: £5.50
less spaghetti
and bread: £1.50
(less spaghetti
and bread: £1.50)
(less ½ bottle red
poison: 75p)

23 June: Sunday midday have five pints of

bitter at pub with beloved who drinks only halves. Lunch on spaghetti bolognese at flat. More love in the afternoon. To the boozer in the evening. This is the life

Drinks: £6 (less spaghetti and bread: £1.50)

28 June: A quiet weekend at Earls Court (if it is possible to have a quiet weekend at Earls Court). On Saturday you go to a theatre and sit in the gallery holding hands just like teenagers

Drinks: £5
Gallery: £3 (less two meals of spaghetti bolognese and bread: £3)

5 July: Another lover's weekend. As it's raining you spend the whole weekend making love in the flat and watching TV

Drinks: £2.95 (less spaghetti and bread: £3)

12 July: It is her birthday. You buy a present. You take her out to an expensive place by the river where you can dine and dance. You buy champagne. But at least you've found out how to avoid parking fines

Gift: £11.40
Dinner: £27.60
Champagne: £9.55

19 July: There was a bit of a row last weekend about you rolling over and going to sleep so you decide to get away from it all with a weekend in Brighton. As you are now living on an advance of office expenses, when the bill arrives you suggest she might like to contribute and of course she says yes immediately – 'I would have insisted anyway' – and hands you £5

Hotel: £35
Meals: £22
Drinks: £9 (less: £5)

26 July: She takes you out to dinner, bless her, ('after all the money you spent on me last weekend'). A nice little Indian place round the corner which seems to specialize in Madras gristle. She gets confused ordering the wine so you pay for

Tip: 70p
Drinks: £1.50

that. She doesn't know much about tipping so you pay for the service charge too

Wine: £3.25 (less gristle: £8.10)

27 July: Maybe it was the gristle but, not only was it all wrong in bed last night, you woke up with a vile hangover. Over breakfast your beloved reveals she is getting a rise of £500 a year and tells you her present salary, which is already bigger than yours

30 July: Meet for drinks. You brood over her pay rise

Beer etc.: £3.90

2 August: Rather argumentative evening in pub about women's rights. Sex refused on grounds of pre-menstrual tension

Drinks: £5.60

16 August: You know it's over. She knows it's over. It's over. You decide to part over coffee in the café round the corner and agree to remain good friends

Coffee: 40p

2 September: You go to a party at a friend's place in Chiswick and you meet this interesting girl who is rather pretty and she is generous and kind and offers you wine when you've drunk your bottle. You ask if you can give her a lift home. . . .

It will be noticed that in the affair just described the happiest days were when least money was being spent. Maximum expenditure is at the start when the man's trying to impress and, later, when things go wrong. Thus Law 76 of Coarse Sex: 'Happiness in an affair is in inverse ratio to the amount of money spent.' Or, as Askew once told a girl, 'Madam, do you realize I could have hired the finest courtesan in Paris for what I have just spent on this unsuccessful evening?'

It has occurred to me that the above diary might be a little biased in favour of the male (cries of 'No, not at all, seems perfectly fair to me.') I have therefore worked out another table of the cost of love as it might affect a girl in a typical affair.

The Price of Love (11)	£	P
7000 feet of spaghetti	9	15
5 gallons bolognese sauce	11	31
24 breakfasts	20	00
Laundry (bed linen)	35	16
Replacement of torn sheets	14	18
Dry-cleaning of blankets over which lover-boy ejaculated	2	50
Replacing wallpaper also ejaculated over by lover-boy	21	76
Gin and whisky at home	22	19
35 gallons of coffee	20	00
New mattress	29	88
Repairing cigarette burn in antique cushion	22	07
Cleaning red wine stain from cream carpet	4	00
Sundry small loans	16	00
Use of phone to call Harry in Australia	33	15
Stolen books	18	46
Replacement of book hurled into fire with cry of 'I won't read that rubbish'	4	95
Contraceptives	11	31
Pregnancy test	5	00
Extra toilet paper ('I like the crisp sort')	1	36

(The above does not include the distress caused by a poisoned thumb obtained from the prick of a needle while darning the loved one's sock.)

7 *Some Problems and Hazards and How to Overcome them*

There is one form of life to which I unconditionally surrender,
Which is the feminine gender. OGDEN NASH

*Common sexual troubles – uncommon sexual troubles – some interesting
positions – sex for the middle-aged – Uncle Walter's dreadful confession*

The course of true love rarely runs smoothly; in fact, as Askew
says, it is more likely to flow like a badly maintained drain, and
the Coarse Lover is bound to encounter many problems on the
way. Some may be his own fault, some those of his partner and
others may be caused by anything from the bed to the landlady.
For instance, a dripping tap ruined one of my own romances. 'I
can't stand that bloody tap!' the girl kept moaning, usually
while I was having an orgasm. It became obsessional. I doubt if
she noticed my efforts at lovemaking. She arose at dawn and
flounced off home 'to get some sleep'. I honestly believe that if
anyone had asked her about the night she would have said,
'Mike never touched me.'

Ever since a girl I was going out with gave me a book on sex
for Christmas I have felt scarcely qualified to issue advice on the
mechanics of love but I firmly believe it's really all in the
woman's mind. After all, on one occasion I apparently gave a
girl a wonderful night of passion without having touched her.
Owing to an excess of whisky I fell asleep as soon as we got into
bed and when I awoke, with a vile headache, she put her arms
round me and said, 'Mike, that was lovely.' Had she dreamed it
all, or was she referring to the bed? Anyway, she seemed just as

happy as other girls, and happier than some, although one girl did write to me, 'We always got on well physically, Mike, it's just that you were such a complete and utter bastard in other directions.' It's typical of the male ego that I kept the letter, with the intention of producing it in front of other women less impressed. 'You are the only man I know who produces a written testimonial after making love,' said one girlfriend.

It is some consolation to Coarse Lovers that the entire World Sex Industry of scientists and researchers and doctors is still arguing about exactly how women are 'satisfied'. They should visit a middle-aged friend of mine who has been described to me by three women as 'like an elderly eunuch in bed' and by two more as 'a wonderful lover'. And they're probably all telling the truth as they found it.

Unfortunately, it is not easy to get sensible advice in time of sexual trouble. I used to play cricket with a chap who confessed under the influence of much beer that he once went to a doctor and said dramatically, 'Doctor, I have become impotent.' The doctor replied, 'So have I.' The advice of friends tends to be based on superstitions such as, 'You want to take iron tablets old chap.' But few people admit to failure. Discussing sexual incompetence is the quickest way I know to clear a bar.

Some write to newspapers or magazines, but I am a little suspicious of the quality of their advice after having been a journalist for many years and having known the writers. I was once on a London newspaper with a woman columnist who was having an affair with a married sub-editor. The romance was so torrid they used to lock themselves in her office and have it off every afternoon after a lunchtime session in the boozer. About 3.30 he would come out all dishevelled and she would slip a fresh piece of paper into her typewriter and write, 'Dear Frantic, I think there is something rather sordid in the way you are carrying on with this married man. Love is more than just having physical sex all the time, dear. . . .'

It may help to identify some common problems of love-making and their causes. For instance, impotence in men is rarely physical. It can be caused by many things from hating your mother to one and a half bottles of gin. Other possible causes may be:

Knocking on wall of hotel room from next door.

Intimate caress by girl with cold fingers.

Woman still has tights on.

Woman has different-coloured hair under each armpit.

Realization that you left the car headlights on.

Bedside phone rings; it is your wife.

Partner rolls over and traps male organ between mattress and her hip-bone.

Woman's false teeth fall out during oral sex.

Frigidity in females is inability to have an orgasm. It may be deep-rooted, or the girl may just find the man a creep in bed. Some of the factors which cause male impotence e.g. sudden arrival of waiter with four-course meal, may also cause frigidity. Another possible source is the fact that the woman's husband died four years ago.

Other typical causes are:

Partner has not shaved for three days.

Man's arousal love-play consists of breathing beer fumes in woman's face and clearing throat.

Uneasy feeling that neither party is using contraception.

When undressed man reminds woman of her father when they came to take him to the old people's home.

Partner picks nose during intercourse.

Another problem is premature ejaculation. However, this is not always an absolute thing. As Askew says, 'All ejaculation is premature.' To some extent, the matter is relative and depends on the girl's reactions. However, the problem can be said to be present if (a) the woman is still in the bathroom cleaning her teeth; or (b) you have not yet got into bed.

So much for the symptoms. Some of the causes may be:

Not having had a chance to make love for six years.

Cat jumps on back and licks buttocks.

Girl commits cunifellingio, a sex act so daring my publishers will not allow me to describe it. In any case I could not do so without ejaculating.

Woman takes two hours to get ready for bed.

You read the underwear adverts in *Vogue* while waiting for woman.

Doctor gives you a fortnight to live.

Partner is your best friend's teenage daughter.

Building collapses.

Another, less common, male sexual trouble is inability to terminate intercourse by having an orgasm. Once again, this could be said to be relative, but the problem is present if the sheets have worn out during the night or if your partner is suddenly discovered to be having breakfast. Causes can include:

Man's organ has got a knot tied in it.

Female organ has a U-turn.

Woman reminds man of his aunt.

Man cannot remember how to have an orgasm.

If insertion is difficult for the man, this could be because his member is badly bent, but is possibly because he is trying to make love to a tear in the mattress. The woman should draw his attention to the fact and gently guide him back into position. If ejaculation has already taken place, you might prefer to sell the mattress. Another reason for difficult insertion could be that the woman is using margarine as a lubricant.

According to most sex manuals one should never apologize for poor sexual performance in any way. I can only say that those who write rubbish like that have never met Melba Macdonald, an Australian girl who used to go out with a flatmate of mine, and who would spend Sunday breakfast loudly discussing my friend's shortcomings in the sort of voice you use to call sheep in the outback. Her favourite phrase, if I remember rightly, was, 'He couldn't fuck his way out of a paper bag. A typical Pom.'

It isn't much use trying to convince a woman like that it was all her fault. But, any apology should be qualified with just a hint of blame on the woman – 'I'm sorry about that, dear. Tell me, have you often had this trouble?'

However there is no need to descend to the ridiculous excuses used by Askew, who used to say, 'I'm afraid the Nazi bullet I got in the war must have worked its way to the groin.' He has not used that recently as it reveals his age.

One of my own greatest sexual problems is forgetting the name of the girl I'm making love to. Admittedly, I am always forgetful in any case. I was once on a television programme where the interviewer, who was quite famous, said, 'Well good-bye and thank you, Michael Green,' and I replied, 'Not at all. Thanks very much . . . er . . . er . . . .' at which point I was mercifully faded out. But it gets worse after sex. I think it must be some sort of guilt. I have a terrible mental blockage which leads to some awful scenes in bed, since women seem to find it rather insulting to be made love to by someone who's forgotten their name. Worse, I sometimes get the wrong name – 'But honestly, I really do care for you Angela . . . .'

'It's not Angela, you fool. It's Sally.'

'Well, whoever you may be, I really do care . . . .' No, a declaration of affection doesn't sound very convincing under those circumstances. And, if I meet the girl next day and cry merrily, 'Hullo . . . er . . . er,' she looks daggers. One of them even hit me with her handbag. I don't blame her.

Since I wrote the above story my old pal Watkins has given me a useful wheeze. He says you should always write the girl's name on your wrist with a ballpoint pen, or else put a piece of paper under the pillow with it written on. Askew says no, you might lose it, you should write the girl's name on her forehead or on the ceiling in lipstick.

However, women can be equally forgetful, unless they're just pretending. I had an affair with one girl who swore I had made love to her some years previously and I know I hadn't. She became sulky and said it couldn't have meant much to me, and I had to pretend that I did remember about it after all.

Sliding out of bed is a frequent hazard. This can be fatal with a heavy partner. Research has shown that 65 per cent of the time the couple fall with the man underneath. It is also a common cause of premature ejaculation. For comfortable lovemaking, don't have nylon sheets. Not only are they slippery but they can cause burns during frantic moments of passion.

Snoring is a big problem, perhaps the biggest sexual hazard of all. It is said that whispering gently, 'Stop snoring,' in the ear of the offender will have a subconscious effect, but my experience is that nothing happens and you get louder and louder until eventually your partner wakes up with a scream and so does the rest of the house. A slight shock, such as sprinkling the forehead with cold water, is also recommended by some. Others prefer a hammer. As snoring is usually caused by sleeping on the back, my own remedy is to encourage my partner to turn on her side by offering to caress her back, or more likely prodding her with my finger, and then wedge her there with my hip-bone. Drastic but effective.

Coitus interruptus is one of the dangers of irregular liaisons. I mean coitus which is interruptus not deliberately but by an outside agency, such as a person knocking on the door. There is a special type of jealous female flatmate, the Dreaded Beldame I call her, who makes a habit of spoiling her friend's enjoyment by interrupting at the moment of truth with some request shouted through the door to borrow a box of matches. Somewhat similar to her is the Eternal Gooseberry, who can be male or female. These people specialize in hanging around and preventing their friends from having it off. Such as the girl who won't go to bed and leave you both in the communal living room alone; or who comes downstairs just when you've started, to get the cigarettes she left behind. Even worse is the man who begs a lift in your car from a party, just when you have persuaded a nice girl to let you take her home, and who reveals a short cut by which you can drop the girl first. He won't give up, he insists on telling you how much more convenient it would be to drop Angela first because you can cut across from here, and in the end he just wears you down.

The Dreaded Beldames are impervious to rudeness, on which they thrive, but may possibly be influenced by bribery and emotional flattery. After all, they're only jealous. A few timely gifts can work wonders, especially if accompanied by a hint, such as, 'I'm giving you this table lighter so you won't have to keep knocking on Jane's door for matches, ha, ha, ha . . . .' I know of no way of thwarting an Eternal Gooseberry short of a .38 bullet.

Talking of coitus interruptus, Askew puts forward the ridiculous theory that fear of discovery lends zest to lovemaking. He should know, for he once had to escape from a Croydon house in his underwear when the husband returned unexpectedly. Askew's solution to the problem of a husband returning without warning is to get out the lawnmower before making love, and after cutting a small area leave it on the lawn. The front door is then locked from the inside to delay the entrance of the husband. If he should be heard arriving, it is the work of a moment to rush into the back garden and start mowing the lawn while the wife unbolts the door and says, 'We didn't hear you. We were cutting the grass.' This has always worked, except for the time when he greeted the husband with a used contraceptive dangling from his trouser pocket.

A man's lack of interest in sex can be caused either by a feeling that sex is a demand or by the fact that his partner has become totally repugnant to him. Sometimes men pass through this phase. If you don't, then that just makes your marriage like everybody else's. Women should not follow conventional advice and try to stimulate the man by dressing provocatively. It only makes it worse. My old Uncle Walter often tells how Aunt Alice tried to tempt him when he lost interest in sex about five days after the wedding and replaced love with whisky. She dressed daringly in a low-cut dress (this was 1938) and put on a record of Al Bowley singing 'Love is the Sweetest Thing' when Walter arrived home.

Apparently Walter's sole comment was, 'Woman, your left breast is hanging out. I should put it back, because it might dangle in the frying pan when you are preparing supper, and you wouldn't enjoy that, I can assure you.'

However, sexual boredom may in some cases be overcome by adding extra physical spice to the lovemaking to stimulate the man and the woman; some positions which will help with this are described in the next chapter. But before indulging in any sexual practice find out how experienced your partner is. If innocent, she may misunderstand your meaning. This comment is sparked off by what happened some years ago when my old pal Watkins clicked with a pretty girl who was blessed with a merry laugh and no brains at all. When they got into bed, the girl suddenly said, 'Let's not make love for a minute. Let's have oral sex.'

Well, you needn't make suggestions like that to old Watkins twice. 'Yes,' he said thickly, the words mutilated by lust, 'let's have oral sex,' and commenced operations. She squawked with fear and jerked away.

'No, no, you don't understand,' she wailed. 'I mean let's lie here and talk about it. That's what it means, doesn't it?'

One of the biggest obstacles to the smooth passage of love is the woman who will insist on making public all her bodily functions – the sort who announces loudly in a crowded restaurant, 'Oh damn, I've got to go to the lavatory again, it's those wretched water pills . . . ' Her periods are as good as advertised in the local paper and, in case anyone doesn't know, she will draw their attention to the fact in conversation; her idea of witty table talk is to discuss her constipation. Such women seem to have a perverse compulsion to discuss these matters just before intercourse, like the girl who said to me, 'Yes, I think it'll be all right to make love. I had a slight discharge this morning but I expect it's all right now. . . . '

I knew one girl who used to display her bodily troubles in large letters on a forward-planning wall-chart which she hung in the kitchen. A typical week was:

Monday: Visit clinic for smear test.
Tuesday: See doctor re discharge.
Wednesday: Get suppositories, Tampax, laxatives and nipple cream.
Thursday: Take sample to family planning clinic. Buy urine tablets.
Friday: Curse.
Saturday: Curse. Mike comes.
Sunday: Curse.

Monday: Curse.
Tuesday: Curse?

Reading this while eating breakfast somehow didn't improve our relationship, although I will admit it was probably my fault for being too squeamish.

Unreasonable jealousy and suspicion are a problem encountered in many long-term relationships. If a girl is determined to be jealous she will be so, no matter what happens. The most innocent remark will be misinterpreted. A friend returned from three months in the Middle East and as he entered the house noticed a strange, sweet smell from a new disinfectant.

'Blimey, what have you been doing?' he inquired innocently. 'The place smells like a Cairo brothel.'

'And how,' demanded his wife icily, 'do *you* know what a Cairo brothel smells like?'

His explanation that he had reluctantly had to enter one to sell them something was not believed. But then no explanation would be. Sometimes I think it would be better deliberately to invite jealousy and say, 'Sorry I'm late home, I stopped to chat up a pretty girl in the park. . . .' At least it'll make you feel better.

Men, of course, are just as jealous as women. And, like women, a jealous man won't believe any explanation, even in the unlikely event of it's being true. In my experience there are only three things to do when the green-eyed goddess takes over your life: 1 Break it off. 2 Break it off. 3 Break it off.

Askew prides himself on his cleverness in disguising his pathetic extra-marital affairs. In fact, his pitiful attempts at cunning are easily seen through by his wife who just ignores it all. 'Jealous?' she told me once. 'When I find a girl's hair on his jacket I sometimes ask myself, "Can a dead bird leave its cage?"'

I asked old Uncle Walter what was the most serious sexual hazard he had ever encountered in his life and he replied, 'Your aunt, my boy.' I explained that was not quite what I meant and he thought for a moment and said it was when he picked up a girl on the Isle of Wight and parked his old Morris on a slipway while they made love in the car. 'Things were just getting interesting,' he said, 'when I noticed that water was pouring into the car. I'd been so preoccupied I hadn't noticed the tide was coming in. I couldn't get her to start so we had to wade to safety and leave the car there. Worse, the girl said she didn't feel like it after that. There is no accounting for women, my boy.'

8 How to Revitalize Your Sex Life and Cope with Getting Older

When a man grows old
And his—grows cold
And the tip of his—turns blue.
And it bends in the middle
Like a one-string fiddle
He can tell you a tale or two. *Eskimo Nell*

Overcoming sexual monotony and wrecking the bedroom – some interesting positions for business executives and others – hazards of growing older – Askew's assault on young nurse

A flagging sex life can be caused by several things. The origins may lie in age, boredom or sheer revulsion, or it's just that you find stamp collecting more exciting and less smelly. However, there are ways in which a drooping relationship can be revitalized, and given new life, always assuming you want it revitalized. Some people would prefer to leave it dormant and I'm not blaming them. Ask your wife before taking unilateral action to restore the flames of passion. She might prefer to sleep of nights.

Sexual monotony can be overcome by frequently changing positions used when making love, according to most authorities. A great deal of research has been done in this field by the expert American team of Masters and Johnson but they appear to have overlooked several novel and stimulating positions which I shall describe later. Perhaps Masters got cramp. But there are other factors which affect sex life, and attention to these areas may produce a change for the better. What will probably happen is that your sex life will be fine but your

ordinary existence will be miserable. Here are some suggestions:

Reduce intake of alcohol. Do not drink during intercourse.

Stop worrying about work. Worry affects the sex drive. Take up
a job which involves less responsibility. You'll probably be
poverty-stricken but it'll be more fun in bed, unless you start
worrying about being poor so much you become impotent.

Get more sleep. As this will probably involve a change of job,
perhaps involuntary, it can be combined with the previous
suggestion.

Diet. Too much weight makes sex difficult. A diet will probably
make it impossible, as you won't have any energy, but it'll do
you good.

Make your wife diet. A much better idea.

Stimulate yourself with erotic literature. Do not, however, look
at the book while actually having intercourse as this is
impolite, not to mention dangerous. If you are really interested, perhaps some of the more exotic photographs could
be reproduced on the pillow or ceiling.

Think of Masters and Johnson while having intercourse. Especially useful in cases of premature ejaculation.

Indulge in fantasy play, viz. wife dresses up as Queen Victoria,
husband as Prince Albert. *Note:* It is essential to enter into
the spirit of the game. It is not fair to lie down on the bed in a
top hat and go to sleep on the grounds that, if Prince Albert
were alive, he would be 160 years old. Another useful fantasy
is for the husband to pretend he is tiptoeing into the bedroom
as an adulterer come to seduce the wife. To make this more
realistic he should wear flashy clothes and brothel-creeper
shoes, which he carries in his hand while he walks on tiptoe.
It is a wise precaution for the wife to make sure it *is* her
husband, and not someone who has just crept into the house,
or the man come to mend the television set. Or perhaps she
won't care anyway.

Feel free to indulge in harmless deviations such as bondage,
whipping, biting, bicycling around the room naked, gnawing
chunks of flesh from each other etc. If indulging in bondage,
remember it is no use tying each other up as then neither

party can move. Keep some iodine handy and leave a key with the neighbours.

Most sex authorities suggest that lovers find out what turns either partner on. The woman might try wearing her son's motorcycling gear for instance. Make sure he doesn't want to ride his motorcycle at the time or you may be interrupted by a cry of, 'Mum, have you seen my leather trousers?' and it would be impracticable to reply, 'Yes, your father's got them wrapped round his John Thomas.' I have just read a sex manual which recommends 'an old prostitute's trick' – the man pulls the woman's panties over his head and wears them while making love. But beware – fifteen cases of suffocation were reported in Sheffield last year. Not a pleasant way to die, Carruthers.

Both man and woman may benefit from keeping fit, we are told. A five-mile jog, followed by a hot bath and a double brandy should solve most sex problems since both will be too tired to bother.

And now here are some unusual positions for making love which may help even the most reluctant sex life spring into new vitality. It will be noted that there is what I call a strong commercial bias in them, in as much as several are designed for use in the office, but they can easily be adapted for the home with a little ingenuity:

The marketing manager: A real commercial favourite, much-favoured by the ladies, and perhaps the most common position of all for lovemaking, although the standard authorities seem to ignore it and my Encyclopaedia of Sex has no mention of it. The woman stands with her back to a large office desk, with one foot in each of the bottom drawers. If necessary, she may prefer to lean backwards over the typewriter. The man approaches by running out of the door of the adjacent office, wearing his hat and perhaps carrying a briefcase or umbrella (see photograph). Sexual stimulus is heightened if the woman holds a notebook and pencil. (NB A pencil should be held sideways to avoid risk of injuring partner.) This position is known in France as '*le patron*'; in Germany as '*der Obergruppenfornikatermeister*'; and in Spain as '*el picador*'. In America it is sometimes called '*the *vice-president.'*

The filing cabinet: In this position the women takes the initiative It is ideally suited to the tired business executive. The man sits in the open drawer of a large metal filing cabinet. (*Note:* If operating at home a chest of drawers or the garbage bin can be used.) The woman stands over him and lowers herself gently down. The woman controls the act of intercourse which is achieved by pushing the drawer in and out with her feet – unless you bribe the office boy to do it. This position is much favoured by women's libbers and office equipment suppliers – indeed, in the USA it is often called '*the Kalamazoo*'. (*Note:* Much added zest is given to the lovemaking if you use the boss's private filing cabinet, preferably the one containing your own personal records.)

The alpine: This is suitable for love in the home. The woman stands on her head on the bed and bends at the hips so her feet touch the wall. The man climbs up the wall (using crampons) and descends from the ceiling with a wild shriek. This position is not recommended by Masters and Johnson, or indeed any-body else, except members of the British Mountaineering Federation. A good eye is essential.

The squash court: One for the connoisseur, this is designed to solve the problem of where to make love when having an office affair in a building where the cleaners come round at five and both parties live out of town. A squash court is hired and both parties dress as for squash. It is more fun if you actually start a game. After a few moments place the ball against the end wall and say to your partner, 'I dare you to pick it up.' Wink as you do so and tear off your shorts with a whoop of triumph. The woman must not straighten up after grasping the ball or harm may result to the man. *Do not use this position in courts with a public gallery.*

The Kamikaze: Definitely one for the young. The man starts from the far end of the bedroom and takes a running dive on to the bed. The woman adopts the best posture she can (crouching in terror is probably as good as any).

The back-to-back position: I have just read a sex manual which actually recommends this, although it fails to give any diagrams, and all I can say is that I don't believe it is possible except for snakes. Suitable for snails, perhaps, or American sex researchers.

POSITIONS FOR SPECIAL SITUATIONS

Many people find the act of love difficult because of the way they or their partners are built. Leaving aside those who have two heads or three legs, obesity is the most common cause of difficulty. I have already made the point that, while diet may help, it may weaken you so much you won't want to make love anyway. However, by adopting certain well-thought-out postures, it is possible for even the most weirdly shaped person to make love.

Thin man and fat girl: The girl lies on her side with one leg wound round the bedpost or some similar fixture and her other foot in her mouth. The man, finding entry impossible, resorts to onanism, after which they both go down to the pub for a drink.

Thin girl and fat man: The girl kneels on the bed with her hands clutching the headboard and tries to bite her knees with her teeth. The man makes love by starting on the floor and clambering towards her from the foot of the bed, grunting occasionally. The danger of this method is that his weight will cause him to sink deep into the mattress and below operational level. In that case he should content himself with sucking the girl's big toe, which will be somewhere near his mouth. NB Beware health hazard. A case of athlete's tongue was reported in Arkansas in 1975.

Fat girl and fat man: Impossible.
Thin girl and thin man: Possible, but noisy.

GETTING OLDER

A decaying sex life is not necessarily a sign of age, although if the male member itself is actually decaying see a doctor at once. It might just be the soap used to wash your underwear. However, age is undoubtedly a sexual problem. The difficulty for men as they get older is not so much Doing It, which they can manage, but Getting It. Often the first signs of approaching age are when a man starts thinking of all the women he's passed up in his life and wishing he hadn't. Although age is a problem it is also, as Askew bitterly remarked, 'the final solution'. The situation is neatly summed up in a parody of Andrew Marvell's poem 'To His Coy Mistress' which Wynford Vaughan-Thomas, the former BBC commentator, composed impromptu on a menu in a pub near Broadcasting House:

> Time's winged chariot poets say
> Warns us to love while yet we may.
> Must I not hurry all the more
> Who's got it parked outside the door?
> For those who sipped love in their prime
> Must gulp it down at closing-time.

I think these are some of the most beautiful and sad words in the English language and they should be pinned over every young woman's bed. Note the closing-time analogy. That was pretty apt, because they threw us out five minutes later.

Unfortunately, in the race to gulp down love before closing time, it's easy for a middle-aged man to mistake the intentions of young girls. A feature of ageing is not that young girls stop being affectionate; they become *too* affectionate. They feel safe with older men and are free with kissing and hugging in public, when they wouldn't dare do the same with somebody younger. One paradox of getting older is that the girls will kiss you more in public and less in private. The danger is that these innocent demonstrations may be mistaken for a come-on.

I recall Askew being nearly thrown out of hospital because he sexually assaulted a nineteen-year-old nurse who he believed to be fond of him. One day he had cramp and the nurse asked if he would like his back massaged. A fatal invitation. Askew's reaction was ecstatic. He gibbered with glee as his pyjama trousers were removed and he was helped on to his face. Askew claimed later that after two minutes he could detect what he called 'an element of enjoyment' in the nurse. 'It was more than a medical duty,' he said later. 'She was giving me an open invitation.' The upshot was that he rolled over and dragged the girl down on to the bed. She called the ward sister and Askew was threatened with sedation.

Had Askew been young, his escapade would have been regarded as an adventure. As it was, he was looked upon as a dirty old man. Yet plenty of girls prefer older men. It's just that older men have to be careful with their advances. Don't assume a young girl is encouraging you unless she is fairly explicit (such as by grabbing your private parts, for instance).

Another sign of age is when girls start to be kind. They can be very cruel to men of their own age but they don't like to hurt older men. When a girl says, 'No, honestly, it's not because you're thirty years older than me . . . no, I really didn't mind your dentures slipping when you kissed me. . . . It's just that I think of you as a *friend* . . .' It is time to look to your muttons (whatever that means). Or jump in the river.

It is also difficult for a man to keep up with changing sexual fashions as he grows older. Until 1950, sexual morality didn't change much, in theory at least. As Uncle Walter put it, 'My boy, in our day no decent girl was supposed to do it outside of marriage, although plenty did. However, your Aunt Alice remained theoretically pure until her wedding night, although I am assured she was easily the biggest cock-teaser in town.'

In the sixties everyone was doing it, in the seventies people were begging not to have to do it so often, and now it seems to be going out of fashion. Promiscuity is no longer the thing. Many girls show a distressing tendency to be able to do without men altogether. At this rate, sexual intercourse will have died out by the end of the century.

Today's youngsters would hardly believe the difficulties experienced by previous generations, with girls expected to be in by ten, landladies who wouldn't allow male visitors, inadequate contraception, and over all a terrible air of furtiveness and illegality. But at least there was an established routine of courtship, unlike today. On the first evening out one was usually allowed to sample the bosom of the beloved; on the second evening further favours were granted; and on the third evening 'yippee' if yippee was to be granted at all. If not, then one either settled down to a long siege, accepted the situation or got another girl. Because of the restrictions, affairs were conducted under incredible difficulties – behind walls, under bushes, down dark lanes. Some men never made love in bed until they were married. Occasionally the novelty was too much for them and they would return with their wives to the fields and bushes. Much lovemaking was carried on in cars, and it is said that girls developed a left breast bigger than their right, since that was the most convenient to reach from the driver's seat.

A further hazard was that hotels frowned on unmarried couples sharing a room, so lovers were reduced to booking under false names. I remember going away for a weekend with my girlfriend and using an assumed name with the girl as my wife. Next day I wanted to ask the desk to call a cab and found *I'd forgotten what name I'd used.* My girlfriend couldn't help – she hadn't even been told whose wife she was supposed to be. Thinking I was very cunning, I asked to see the register and while searching for a clue noticed an old pal and his wife – the Pearsons – had booked in. I hurried to their room, banged on the door and shouted, 'Peter, Sue, let me in, it's Mike Green.' There was a pause and the door was opened by my girlfriend, looking very puzzled. It then dawned on me that I'd registered in my old pal's name. We were Mr and Mrs Pearson.

It was even worse on the continent, with the couple producing two passports containing different names and demanding a double room from some suspicious madame in a remote village in France. The girl was always addressed heavily as 'Madame', followed by a snort of disapproval, and the woman would follow the frightenend pair around with an intense stare as if to say, 'Don't you dare desecrate the Hôtel du Centre by having illicit sex.'

Coarse lovers should face age boldly. Somewhere there's a perverted female who's got a thing about baldness. As Askew once boasted, 'Nature gives you an extra inch after you're forty,' although his wife spoiled the effect by snarling, 'Yes, and in your case it's the soft bit in the middle.' Sometimes Sheila is rather tough on poor old Jack. I remember he was once complaining that the living room door handle was stiff and she snapped, 'In that case it's the only bloody thing in this house that is.' However, as I say, they rub along together in their own way.

There are two views about the advisability of sex in middle and old age. One is that a young mistress keeps a man young. Against that is the fear of 'dying on the job' which haunts everyone over forty-five. It's no empty threat when your heart's pumping madly, your head's spinning and your young partner is asking, 'Are you all right? Why are you retching like that?' These days Askew is so terrified that he will not make love in a strange house without first leaving a note on the dressing table addressed to the local coroner.

Resist the temptation to act younger than you feel. Don't force yourself to be with it. Just gently remind your young friend from time to time that in the long run we are all dead and we all go the same way home. She won't thank you, but it'll make you feel better and might damp down that eternal bloody optimism of youth.

Choose things you can do gracefully in middle age with a young companion. Swimming might not be a good idea, especially if you have to be helped out of the pool. But sailing is ideal for the middle aged, who are often the only people who can afford it. Contrary to popular belief, it need not involve much physical effort, and the sea-dog-type clothes sailors wear are rather flattering to a mature man. So is the show of authority and the barking of commands. Tennis doubles is another fine sport for the mature man to play with a younger girl. But don't play singles at anything (except golf). I still sometimes play badminton with a twenty-five-year-old girl, and she now says I am not to rely on her for mouth-to-mouth resuscitation when I turn blue and lean against the wall.

And, whatever happens, after the age of forty-five don't try to jump the net if you win. Especially at badminton. On the other hand there's no need to crawl *under* the net after a game of tennis, like Askew does. Just walk round the side.

Be careful when reminiscing about the past. Young people have little sense of period and tend to lump William the Conqueror, Stalin and Elvis Presley all together into a vague limbo called 'the old times'. A reference to the fact you were alive at the same time as Hitler may be interpreted as meaning you are ninety-five years old. A recent survey revealed that two-thirds of the eighteen-year-olds questioned thought Napoleon was somebody from the First World War. So don't turn your hat sideways, whatever you do.

Avoid showing an obsession with young flesh. Pretend it means nothing to you. Tell your young partner you usually prefer older women. Try not to slaver in the salad when you eat together. Don't sniff the armpit of her old school uniform. Askew will never get a young mistress, I'm afraid, as these days his obsession with youth is such that, when playing tennis with a young partner, he warns her, 'Don't bend down for the ball whatever you do my dear, or I may be inflamed beyond control.' This does not endear the girls to him and it wrecks the tennis as well.

To conclude this section, a final warning on sex and age: never indulge in oral sex after the age of sixty-five unless you want to die with a beautiful smile on your face.

9 International Interlude

Hand me my capsules. BARON DE GAUTIER

It's love which stops the world going round properly – horrible misunderstanding in Germany – fallacy of the Scotsman's kilt – the unpleasantness in America

One of the greatest fallacies about sex is that the language of love is international, that love between man and woman breaks down all the barriers between different nations. I only wish it were true, but I remember with pain years spent abroad trying to chat up foreign girls without a word of any common language. What chance has a man got when he's reduced to burbling gibberish like, 'England. England. Me from England. Understand?' and making absurd gestures with the hands as if trying to tie two bits of string together.

Another difficulty is that the pair have to reduce complicated emotions and subtleties to jerked phrases. I remember meeting a lovely German girl who rather unusually knew not a word of English. What I wanted to say was how pretty she looked, and what did she do for a living, and did she ever go to the opera, and would she like a stroll by the lake tomorrow afternoon? In the end, I was reduced to barking loudly, '*Ich liebe dich* . . . me . . . you . . . love' (placing hand on chest and groaning). 'Love. *Der heart. Das heart.* For you. *Faschtein love, nein?*' I must have looked like something out of a bad musical comedy. She, too, probably wanted to say something noncommittal, and here was this buffoon making a noise as if he was about to vomit and asking her to say she loved him for ever. In the end she said yes to everything and I was delighted, until I realized she didn't understand a word.

I am not alone. We have all been reduced to idiots by the language barrier at one time or another. And I refuse to believe that any girl who understands the universal 'You jig-a-jig?' is the sort of girl one would wish to jig-a-jig with. The language of love is not universal and Coarse Lovers would be advised to be careful when they meet a foreign girl unless they can get down to the physical nitty-gritty immediately without the aid of words. And even that is not advisable unless they are familiar with the local culture. After wreaking your will on a Mexican maiden it is rather late to discover that in that remote region they still castrate men who seduce girls.

With regard to this language difficulty, I believe the best solution is to stick to your own tongue, unless you have more than a few words of the other language. (The great Dr Johnson insisted on speaking in either English or Latin when abroad, as he believed a man looked foolish struggling to speak a foreign language and it was better not to be understood than to look a fool.) A flow of English reinforced by gestures will impress a girl more than pitiful attempts at her own language like '*Donnez-moi your hand*' or '*Ich want to schlaffen mit you.*' That's why Italians get on so well with foreign women – their own language is so liquid and beautiful it sounds as if they're making love even when they ask the way to the lavatory.

Extra care is needed if you think you know the language or have a smattering of it. I shall not easily forget the time when I often used a phrase which obviously puzzled a French girl and, when I checked later, I discovered I had been saying, 'I want to lay an egg.' No wonder she rejected all my advances. She must have thought I was bonkers.

Once a relationship has been established, the language problem often fades, of course, although I always think of a friend who received a letter from his Italian girl which ended, 'I have had such lovely feelings of you. . . .' A rather less happy mix-up happened to someone I know who tried to chat up a Danish girl in Copenhagen. He returned to England carrying what he thought was a loving message from her written on a scrap of paper in a bar, and gave it to a Danish-speaking colleague to translate. It said simply, 'You are an English turd and I hate you.'

Traditions have developed over the years about the sexual habits of various nations and, like so many of these traditions, they are not founded on fact but ideas formulated many years ago. I mean beliefs such as Englishmen still have that Paris is the place for 'getting it' – a fallacy that dates from the time of Edward VII, I believe. In fact, French girls are rather prim and prudish by English standards, as many a drunken Englishman has discovered. As for club hostesses and other professionals, they are the same the world over. To help Coarse Lovers recognize the most notorious fallacies about international sex, I have compiled a table on national myths and differences:

THE SCOTS

Tradition: Scotsmen are sturdy and tough. The action of the wind blowing up their kilts has strengthened their loins to an incredible degree. They are strong, silent and effective lovers.

Truth: Most Scotsmen have such a Calvinistic sense of guilt about sex that they are incapable of making love without having a drink. Unfortunately, it is a national failing that no Scotsman can ever stop at one drink, so they are equally incapable of making love because of complete intoxication. A Scottish Health Council poster shows a wife sitting up in bed as her husband arrives home the worse for wear from the pub and saying bitterly, 'Ah see you've had sixteen pints of yon contraceptive again.' Who is a mere Englishman to disagree with that?

THE ENGLISH

Tradition: Englishmen are cold and inhibited. They do not know how to treat women with gallantry. They prefer male company and live on boiled cabbage.

Truth: The randiest nation on earth. Englishmen spend their entire lives looking for it. Unfortunately, it is quite true they don't know how to treat women, but English girls are so used to it that by now they would scarcely know any different.

Otherwise the English would be the most unsatisfied nation in the world. They do not live on cabbage but on potato crisps and beer.

THE WELSH

Tradition: Sneaking, honey-tongued seducers.

Truth: Most Welsh lads are devoted to their old mam. After a brief period in their youth of intense fornication – most of which is conducted in the open air – they marry a younger replica of their mam and live nearby her. Welsh contraception is the worst in Europe, so the bride is probably pregnant. After a while, the novelty of marriage wears off but by then it is too late to do anything about it, and they are under the thumb of the formidable Welsh matriarchy – the strongest union of women in the world.

THE IRISH

Tradition: Years of suppression by the Catholic Church and economic problems have left the men with no desire to marry and the girls too inhibited to have affairs outside of marriage, so the population is falling.

Truth: It is not suppression by the Catholic Church which is the true threat to the Irish birth rate but suppression by immense quantities of stout. Given the choice between a girl or a Guinness, most Irishmen will go for the Guinness first and then it's too late, since no Irishman will quit the field while still sober. Irish girls are quite uninhibited and sophisticated sexually, provided they can catch a partner between drinks. They have to be quick. It is an education to watch an Irish girl working on a man in a brief moment of time before he goes back to the party/dance/bar for more stout:

'Shaun! Shaun! Will ye stop staggering for a moment? Now listen Shaun . . . Mother of God, he's fallen down again. Shaun! Shaun! Get up, will ye? Now listen, I want ye to come back to my place for a cup of coffee with Maire and the others. . . . No Shaun, don't go back in there yet, just listen will ye? Now Shaun – Jesus, he's fallen down again – Shaun, lean against me will ye, now I want you to promise you'll come back with the others to my place . . . promise . . . promise . . . seal it with a kiss . . . Christ Almighty, he's missed me lips. . . . No, Shaun, here's me face, it's the wall you're pecking at. . . .'

If this sort of thing fails, their last resort is to catch him coming out of mass on Sunday morning.

Alas, Irish girls are incurably romantic and have a death wish as regards men. They cannot resist fiddlers and priests, and since the one are usually drunk and the others celibate *and* drunk, the chances for girls are slim. An Irish girl's dream is a fiddler who has been thrown out of a monastery for lechery, but there aren't many of those.

THE FRENCH

Tradition: Frenchmen are courteous, charming and irresistible to women. They have a special relationship to *l'amour* which other nations cannot possibly match, a relationship summed up in the phrase 'ooh-la-la'. Love is their sole hobby and often their profession as well.

Truth: Most Frenchmen these days are too busy making money to pay much attention to love. When not making money they watch television or commit suicide.

THE SPANISH

Tradition: The Spanish are cruel, passionate lovers, who dominate women.

Truth: Most Spaniards live under the thumb of an immensely fat wife. Typical is the man who used to run a beach café on my last holiday on the Costa Brava. He was a wizened little man with a huge moustache, and every time his enormous wife called from the kitchen he rolled his eyes to the ceiling in despair before doing exactly what she wanted.

THE ITALIANS

Tradition: The archetypal Latin lovers, the great dark-eyed sweepers-of-women-off-their-feet into strong arms with honeyed words of love and passion, *carissima mia* etc. etc.

Truth: Most Italians are rather inhibited and frustrated and have to make do with bottom pinching as a substitute for sex. They frequently come to marriage with problems caused by ignorance, fear and the need to prove themselves a full-blooded Italian male. At an early age they abandon sex for wine.

THE SWEDES
Tradition: The Swedes do it all the time, even in buses or on trains, but preferably beside mountain lakes. They think of nothing else. The whole of Sweden is one vast heaving mass of sexual intercourse, and its main industry is making pornographic films. The chief export is nymphomaniac *au pair* girls.

Truth: Swedish women are rather puritanical and home-loving. There is a great deal of promiscuity between the ages of sixteen and twenty (hence the legend of the *au pair* girl), after which they seem to have worked it all out of their systems and settle down to a conventional life. A surprisingly high percentage of Swedish girls are said to be frigid. After a few years of marriage they become like middle-aged German *hausfraus* and bustle around their spotless kitchens tut-tutting about young girls today.

THE AUSTRALIANS
Tradition: Australian men are not interested in women's company, although they enjoy the physical side of sex as much as anybody else. They prefer to gather in male groups and drink beer and discuss sport while the females gather together at the other end of the room.

Truth: Australian men are not interested in women's company, although they enjoy the physical side of sex as much as anybody else. They prefer to gather in male groups and drink beer and discuss sport while the females gather together at the other end of the room.

THE AMERICANS
Tradition: 'The Yanks really know how to treat a girl.'

Truth: Americans treat girls just like anybody else. It's just that back home the women insist on being treated well and, since nothing on earth is more powerful than the combined force of American womanhood (except the Welsh matriarchy), it becomes a habit. Americans also have the advantage of usually having more money than other people. If you meet an American without any money, you will find he doesn't treat women any better than an Englishman does.

THE AFRICANS

Tradition: African Negroes have tremendous sexual potency and vitality. All white women have a subliminal desire to be made love to by a Negro.

Truth: I am indebted to Sigi, an old pal with whom I used to play cricket, and who was himself a Negro from Nigeria, for the explosion of this myth. 'Man,' he said, 'they've got those great big black choppers and they're so long they can't get them upright. Why do you think they've killed nearly every damn rhinoceros in Africa? To get powdered rhino horn for an aphrodisiac, that's why. Can you get powdered rhino horn here in Birmingham? No. And why? 'Cos the folks here, they ain't impotent, that's why, there ain't no market for the stuff. It don't take so much energy man, to raise those little English choppers.'

Thank you Sigi, and I'm sorry to call you by your nickname, but I never did learn to pronounce the full title. You may have been a lousy cricketer, but you're a splendid philosopher.

THE JAPANESE

Tradition: Love is a great art-form in Japan, where geisha girls are trained for years in the little ways of pleasing men.

Truth: The modern Japanese seem to excel at watching other people do it – you just need to go into any strip show in any capital of Europe to see that. One gets the impression Japanese men are too busy photographing it ever to get round to doing it for themselves, and in any case the camera would get in the way. Geisha girls are now trained in the little ways of pleasing tourists and can process a credit card.

To round off this section, a good example of misunderstanding national cultures comes from my old pal Watkins, who was sent to America on business. He had been warned so much about the terrible tribe of New York hookers that he greeted all female approaches with terror. so when a group of women burst into the bar of his hotel and began leering at him, he hurriedly moved to the other end of the room; when two or three sat down at his table, he hastily got up; and when finally cornered by a pretty blonde who offered him a drink, he fled to his room.

In the morning he proudly told the desk clerk how he had successfully fought off the hookers.

'Hookers, nothing.' said the clerk. 'They wuz a sales convention. They come here every year. If you ask me, bud, you were the only man in the hotel who didn't make it. Pete over there had two.'

Next evening Watkins eagerly patrolled the bar, but the convention was over.

10 The Wedding and Other Gruesome Stories

The wedding guest, he beat his breast
For he heard the loud bassoon. COLERIDGE

Miseries of the wedding — funerals much more enjoyable — how to avoid unpleasantness in church — horrors of reception — Askew offends the entire company

A book on sex would be incomplete without a reference to what is a frequent outcome of the business, namely marriage. As a bachelor, I must admit I prefer funerals to weddings. For one thing everyone is much more cheerful, the food is better and the drink much more plentiful. Also funerals tend to be held at sensible times, whereas weddings are held at indigestible hours such as 3.30 in the afternoon. Who wants to drink warm sherry and eat paste sandwiches at that time? Apart from anything else, one does not have to hire special clothes for a funeral. It is monstrous to make people hire morning dress for a wedding. I make it a rule never to attend any such wedding, unless the bride's father volunteers to pay the hire charge, which he never does. The only exception I make to this rule is if I have slept with the bride. After all, there *is* a code.

It is highly significant that clergymen rarely charge for funerals but positively rook the public for weddings. This shows the official opinion of the Church on the merit of the two services. And who would not prefer the funeral service with its majestic phrases about ashes to ashes to the banalities of the wedding and its archaic references about obeying and 'with my body I thee worship'. I remember bursting into laughter at that bit when Askew got married. The thought of Sheila Askew worshipping her husband's skinny frame was too much for me.

Weddings bring out the worst in people, whereas funerals bring out the best. At funerals people are sympathetic and kind to each other (after all, anyone could be next). Later, after the drink, the talk is lively but sensible, on serious matters such as the World Cup or the Open Golf Championships. Weddings are full of people in silly hats babbling frothy, stupid conversation, and later the hearty set start those dreary practical jokes such as tying kippers on the exhaust of the groom's car or phoning the honeymoon hotel and changing the booking to two single rooms (ha, ha, ha).

However, there are certain wheezes which the Coarse Lover can use to ensure that a wedding is less dreary than usual, even if it doesn't match up to his grandmother's funeral. As regards stupid pranks, these are caused by boredom which originates from standing around in fancy dress trying to catch the eye of a waitress dishing out thimblefuls of cheap wine. Paradoxically, the more booze that is supplied, the less there will be a tendency to merry japes. Who wants to waste time tying kippers to an exhaust pipe when there's booze by the bucketful at the reception? It is significant that the worst outbreak of practical joking I ever saw was at a temperance wedding with vast jugs of lemonade on the table. Within half an hour everybody had drunk five pints of it and there was nothing else to do, at which time Satan made work for idle hands and mayhem broke out. JUST MARRIED was sprayed over every vehicle in sight, wheels were removed and someone lit a fire in the best man's top hat. Yet all were dreadfully and completely sober.

The stage management of the wedding service is important. One of the great difficulties of a church service is that the whole thing is based on the idea that these two people have never made love to each other and are now being licensed to do so. In fact, the whiter the wedding, the more emphasis on bridesmaids, the 23rd Psalm and orange blossom, the more sex has usually taken place. So there is the problem that perhaps half the male guests have slept with the bride (occasionally the bridegroom is the only one that hasn't). Therefore all guests who have had intercourse with the bride must be placed on the groom's side. It is not fair to have a solid phalanx of muscular young men all down one side of the church behind the bride, together with her boss and the sales manager. By some coincidence, the best man always seems to be one of the bride's former lovers, while the groom has usually had a couple of the bridesmaids. Girls who have slept with the groom should sit on the *bride's* side. (*Note*: If the groom and the best man have slept together, cancel the wedding.)

Do not invite anyone who has had an affair with bride or groom which has ended in bitterness. Otherwise the ceremony may be marred by a loud voice in church saying, 'I had her once and I didn't like it,' or 'She doesn't know what she's letting herself in for.' By not inviting people with a grievance you will also spare the happy couple the possible embarrassment of barbed remarks at the reception, such as 'I'm afraid you will find he snores a lot in bed, dear. . . .'

One curse of getting married is the traditional stag party. If held the night before the wedding it results in a bridegroom who has to be supported to the altar and who is shaking so much he can't get the ring on the girl's finger. That is apart from the fact that his testicles might still be black from the boot polish his merry friends at the rugby club applied the previous evening. Another hazard of the stag night is the regret the bridegroom feels for his lost bachelor days, as he hears the boys planning what to do after the wedding, and how they will take out the girls, and he realizes that in theory at least he is only going to take out one girl for the rest of his life. Many a divorce is born at the stag night bachelor party.

Do not display presents at the reception. This can obviously cause odious comparisons and it is embarrassing to display ten teapots or four salad servers. The guests should be encouraged to give things that won't last. These days any permanent wedding presents such as cutlery will probably have to last through two or even three marriages and dividing the spoils can be difficult, especially when sentiment is involved. I have seen my most valuable gifts scattered from home to home as the couples break up, form new liaisons, and perhaps break up again. I've felt like asking for them back sometimes. After all, they were supposed to be wedding gifts, not pawns in a divorce settlement. However, this difficulty can be avoided by giving things that will wear out eventually, such as sheets, towels, a crate of wine, or even a year's supply of washing powder.

If possible, try to do the catering yourself. It isn't difficult to match the efforts of the normal outside caterer. They seem to double price everything and even then ration it out. They have a recipe for making sandwiches which are actually stale before they've finished buttering the bread. All white wine is warmed in portable ovens. Caterers also employ a specially trained staff of old crones who have the remarkable ability to glide around without serving anybody. The only way to get served is to snatch a glass off a passing tray, and even then they give you a withering look and say icily, 'Did you want a drink, *sir*?' If possible have the reception at home. The money saved will easily pay for an extension to the house or the hire of a marquee.

Caterers, by the way, seem to push up the price for weddings, assuming expense will not matter. This was first pointed out to me by Uncle Walter, and he claims to have made use of the knowledge on the marriage of his eldest daughter ('I shall never get over the disgrace of having a piece of human scum like a bank manager as a son-in-law,' Walter told me). In view of what he felt about his son-in-law, he determined to do things on the cheap and rang up a local firm. 'We are burying my old grandmother on Saturday,' he said, 'And I would be glad if you could do the catering. There will be about fifty mourners present after the service. . . .'

Not only did they quote Uncle Walter a cheaper price than for a wedding but they were considerate and polite, as to a bereaved person. 'I shall definitely go back there when your aunt dies,' he said afterwards. I think the waitresses were a bit surprised when a white cake appeared and the mourners all turned up wearing carnations but otherwise everything went splendidly. 'All wasted on that son-in-law,' said Uncle Walter bitterly.

Speeches are a big problem at a wedding. The mere fact it's a wedding seems to have an awful effect on speakers, who feel compelled to make sniggering jokes about troubles being little ones when everybody knows the happy couple have been living together for six months. The only laughs at wedding speeches are the unintentional ones. I am thinking of the time the bride's uncle droned on for hours about how they never thought little Daphne would ever get married, she was such a shy girl. In fact, as the uncle said, 'We didn't think she ever had it in her.' There was a ghastly pause during which someone could distinctly be heard whispering, 'Well, she will tonight.'

I shall never forget Askew's speech when he was best man to a mutual friend of ours. He stood up with difficulty, holding a glass of champagne which he spilled over the bride's head, swayed for a moment and sat down with an idiot grin on his face. Eventually he was persuaded to stand up again and he commenced his toast to the bridesmaids, and indeed anything else he could find.

His first joke would have been just about passable in the bar of a rugby club at 11.30 on Saturday night. His second was received in stony silence, and no wonder as it contained every known obscenity in the English language. As for his third, I could see the ghastly punchline coming a mile away; we could all see it coming, and no one was looking forward to it. But remorselessly Askew dragged on, 'And so you see when they got into the bathroom – no, that's not right, I mean the bedroom, ha, ha, ha, what would they be doing in the bathroom? Well, when they got into the bedroom, the man said. . . . No, wait a minute I forgot to say that *before* they went upstairs the man had asked the girl if she was double-jointed . . . that's important you see. . . .' Eventually he reached the terrible conclusion and paused for laughter. None came, although an elderly aunt got up and marched out. Then the bride's father arose, and with a shout of 'You filthy animal, how dare you use language like that in front of my daughter?' launched himself at Askew who was standing there leering at everybody. The fact that Askew was utterly shotters saved him from injury as he collapsed under the assault and both fell beneath the table, which hampered the father's blows. Even so it took three men to part them.

But then Askew always disgraces himself on these sort of occasions. I have told in *The Art of Coarse Drinking* how at a christening party he dragged the vicar round the house pointing out the various places where he believed his children had been conceived. None of these places was the bedroom and they included behind the bathroom door and at the kitchen sink. As Sheila Askew says, 'That man is too idle to get into bed to do it.' The strangest place of conception could not be shown. Askew's eldest daughter is believed to have been conceived before marriage on the third fairway of Walton Heath golf course. 'And I never paid the green fee,' says Askew triumphantly.

The happiest wedding I have ever attended was one in which I had a deep personal interest, since the bride was five months pregnant and I was responsible. It had all begun at a party when a friend came up and said, 'Mike, I've just met the most smashing redhead and would you please lend me a Durex?' So I did, but accidentally gave him an old one that had been optimistically lurking in a far corner of my wallet for some years. My friend vowed to return the favour – I don't know if he intended to give me the same one back – and went off to his redhead. A few months later I got an invitation to the wedding. The protective had obviously not survived its long confinement in my wallet and the wedding was a shotgun affair.

The bride, who was a well-built girl, was so pregnant she had difficulty in getting up the aisle alongside her father, who was not exactly slim. But, that difficulty aside, it was a splendid service, conducted by a priest who was a relative of the groom and who knew the circumstances. Without a flicker on his face he beamed down on the young mother-to-be and delivered a splendid sermon on the importance of chastity before marriage. At the reception all was happiness and jollity, and why not, since the happy pair's union had been blessed immediately, as you might say, and there was double cause for celebration. The bride and groom thanked me with tears in their eyes, as well they might, and even the priest came over and shook hands and said, 'I hear you're the terrible man responsible for starting all this.' Friends, I feel kinda humble.

The happy pair have now been married for many years and have a large family for which, as the father says, I am basically responsible. It is pleasant to know one has not lived in vain.

Incidentally, it might be asked what a Catholic was doing asking for contraceptives. I raised this very point with my friend and he replied, 'It's only a sin to use contraception if you're married. If you're single you're not supposed to be doing it at all.'

11 Parting is Such Sweet Sorrow, or Something

Oh, I am sick to see you, will you never let me be?
You may be good for something but you are not good for me.
Oh, go where you are wanted, for you are not wanted here.
And that was all the farewell when I parted from my dear.
A. E. HOUSEMAN *A Shropshire Lad*

*The end of the affair – Askew's terrible experience in a public
lavatory – how to write a goodbye letter – how to receive a
goodbye letter – a slight misunderstanding – Job's comforters –
onward, ever onward*

The parting of two people in a relationship is usually painful
for one and a relief for the other. ('Rubbish,' says Uncle
Walter, who is peering over my shoulder again. 'Parting from
a spouse must be the happiest day of your life. I know I look
forward to it almost as much as your aunt does.') In Coarse
Sex the parting is often especially painful, however, since the
man has a suspicion the girl has found herself a better man.
Thus the Coarse Lover should prepare himself in advance for
ways of dealing with the end of an affair. This preparation
should start as soon as it begins. It's not a bad idea, as you are
shaving the morning after first making love to a girl, to ask,
'How is this all going to end? And how am I going to get out of
it?' Perhaps a trifle pessimistic, but then life is like that.

Some Coarse affairs just last one night so there is no warning
of approaching doom. You come into the office/tennis club/
saloon bar and smirk at the girl who was so enthusiastic for
you last night, and whisper, 'Coming back to my place again
for a cup of coffee?' and she turns on you with a freezing glare
and says no thank you, and you realize that, as far as she is
concerned, it was just a One Night Job. At this shattering
blow to the ego there is a tendency to blame yourself, to ask,
what did I do wrong? In fact there might be nothing wrong. It

is unlikely she is turning you down on the evidence of one night. Even a TV set on approval gets longer than that. If you were totally repulsive she wouldn't have made love in the first place. Just tell yourself she must have a hang-up.

The shortest affair I ever experienced was when I took out a girl who returned home with me and, after we had been in bed for half an hour, she got out and insisted on going back to her own place. I couldn't get any coherent reason from her. Obviously the poor girl was ill emotionally. I mean no girl would walk out just like that . . . (keep talking, keep talking). Seriously I do believe it was the bed. It slopes sideways and she kept falling out.

But usually a woman throws a man over for no reason at all, except that unalterable Law of Female Nature, viz: 'I don't know why I did it.' Half the time women go around doing things to men without knowing what they're doing, whether it's nice things like suddenly buying you a drink or nasty ones like standing you up.

Never, therefore, look for logic or reason in the separation. The only certain thing is that the reason given for parting is never the real one, which lies buried deep in the girl's ovaries and is not even known to her. Though it is doubtful if any girl could ever match Askew's bizarre reason for leaving a person. He claims he left a girl because he found her name written up in a public lavatory with the inscription 'For a good time ring 5672 and ask for Shirley.' As Askew said, 'No man worth his salt could have gone out with her after that.'

I'm glad I mentioned Askew because it ought to be said that male reasons for leaving women can be just as illogical as women's for leaving men and based on some mysterious force outside our control.

Always be on the watch for signs of a partner's losing interest. One of the first is that, instead of jealously watching every move, she actively encourages you to enjoy yourself without her.

'Why don't you go down to the pub and play darts with the boys?' she says. Or else, 'You never seem to play golf these days. . . . Why don't you take Maureen to the cinema and I'll watch telly. She'd love to go with you.'

Another sign of impending doom is when a partner starts buying you things. If a woman insists on paying for a meal she's guilty about something. Frequently you will collect your cards during the meal. Girls might like to note that the same applies to men. If a well-established partner suddenly starts showering his mate with gifts, he's being unfaithful.

Eventually a woman cannot resist telling her man about her new affair, but she has to do it indirectly. 'You know Ted Matthews?' she says rather off-handedly. 'He's that tall, rather dishy chap in the sales department. I've been seeing a bit of him recently – just for a few drinks in the pub at lunch – and he's an awfully interesting chap. Do you know he goes gliding at weekends?' A formula like that seems to satisfy the hardy organ that does duty as a woman's conscience, and she now feels she has 'told you'. What she is really saying, of course, is, 'I am having an affair with Ted Matthews. We are doing it at lunchtime. And, if I haven't made that plain to you, then you are an even bigger fool than I took you for.'

If you are stupid enough to ignore the storm signals, she will just get more and more bitchy and unreasonable until she goads you into a filthy temper and throws you over for Ted Matthews, saying she couldn't continue with someone who was so unpleasant.

The worst kind of splitting-up is when something suspicious is going on and nobody will admit it. I have already referred to the horrors of jealousy. Once you reach the stage of trying to justify a partner's actions, it is time to quit.

The brain goes round in circles: 'I suppose it is just possible that when I found her in bed with Ted they were only testing the mattress. . . . Perhaps she really did stand me up because it was raining and not because she went out with someone else. . . . It *might* not have been Charlie's french letter I found under the bed . . . it could have belonged to the landlord, as she said. . . .' That way madness lies, as King Lear put it, and he was a man familiar with female perversity.

It is useless to ask a girl to explain her infidelity or to justify it. She will only give an explanation that is totally ridiculous, such as saying she had been playing Scrabble when you **saw** her leaving a man's flat at 4.00 a.m. A sure sign of guilt, though, is when a girl takes refuge in virtue: 'Surely you don't think I'm the sort of girl who would . . . ?' The use of that phrase is as good as an admission. In short, there is no point in seeking explanations. And girls find the same, too. It is useless for a woman to demand an explanation of the lipstick stain on her partner's collar; she will only receive some drivel about it's being tomato sauce.

Don't waste time on vigils to catch the guilty pair. I remember passing a friend on a rainy night huddled against the railings outside a house. I stopped the car and asked if he wanted a lift. 'No thanks,' he said. 'I'm waiting for Betty to come out of *that man's* house and then I am going to confront her.' Well, I didn't like to probe so I passed on to the pub and, when I returned at about eleven o'clock, who should I see but my friend still glued to the railings and looking a bit the worse for wear. I offered him a lift again, but he declined. 'They must finish soon,' he groaned. 'She can't stay all night because she's supposed to be sleeping with me.' So I drove off. In the morning I happened to drive past the house and saw Betty and a man leave hand in hand. It was about 8.15. There was no sign of my pal so I rang him. It turned out he had given up in disgust at 3.00 a.m. It has always been my ambition to confront a guilty pair as they leave a house together but I'm sure I wouldn't know what to say. I'd probably slink by muttering, 'Good morning.'

Once a parting is decided upon, a method of conveying the decision must be chosen. This isn't as easy as it sounds. If you rely on finding a suitable opportunity to mention the subject you will never get round to it. My old pal Watkins went out with a girl for three years because he never had the courage to discuss splitting up. When he eventually managed to make the break, she said she'd felt the same for three years but was as cowardly as him.

Some lucky people actually have the courage to say calmly to someone, 'By the way, dear, I'd like to have a little chat with you sometime.' There's no need to mention the subject –

it is implicit. I can never do that. I have got as far as, 'By the way, dear. . . . ' but, if the girl looks apprehensive or threatening, I switch the subject to something else. Then I wait for a row to develop so I can use that as a stimulus ('All right, if that's the way you feel about it. . . .'). Unfortunately, if you *want* a row, there won't be one unless you are nasty enough to start it, and even then it's almost impossible. Of course, if you don't want an argument they start easily enough.

Lord Russell, the philosopher, parted from his wife on a bicycle ride. He simply said, 'I have decided to leave you.' But he was a philosopher.

Despite the old adage, 'Wrong no man, write no woman,' for many the only way of communication is the traditional Dear John letter of farewell, which should be posted through the letterbox of the beloved while she is out. Do not trust it to the ordinary mail because it is one of the Laws of Coarse Sex that, upon delivering a farewell letter, a Coarse Lover decides he doesn't want to leave the girl; he sees all her virtues, she suddenly becomes the most desirable object on earth. If the letter is posted, he may ring up and tell the girl to ignore any letter from him or have it intercepted. Do not try to recover a goodbye letter from inside the front door by dangling a piece of string with gum on the end through the letterbox (as Askew did once). Leave the house immediately before you have a chance to change your mind. Ideally, you should leave town as well.

My old pal Watkins always used to go and stay at the same hotel to avoid retracting his decision. It was in Cheltenham, where he had some business calls. They got to know him quite well. 'Been having trouble again sir?' the barman would inquire as Watkins tottered in, his brow creased in pain, and Watkins would say yes, and he was not to be allowed near a telephone that night. During the evening he would pour out his soul to the barman and be helped to bed, dead to the world, mumbling the name of his girlfriend. Next day he started life afresh, the horrors of parting over.

A further advantage of leaving town for a short spell is that one is spared unpleasant scenes if the letter provokes anger. I once broke off an affair just before a trip to Leeds and on returning to my house found the word

SHIT

carved on the front door in letters two inches high and a quarter of an inch deep. No prizes for guessing who did it. But what if I'd been at home? The letters might have been carved on my chest. Incidentally the word was impossible to obliterate and I had to have a new door.

This is all very well if the couple aren't living together, but what if they are? It looks a little odd to drop a letter to the girl through the door when you live in the same house. When Askew lived with a girl before he got married, he tried to break it off by leaving half-finished letters of farewell all over the house. Unfortunately the girl was too polite to read them. She kept handing them back, saying, 'I've found another of your half-finished letters on the table. I wish you'd be more careful – it might be something private.' In the end, Askew left town, and posted his letter. That is probably the best thing to do if you are too cowardly to face the girl. But take any valuables with you. Askew returned to find his belongings in a heap on the front lawn.

The ideal farewell letter should be affectionate, regretful and kind to the partner's emotions. Don't say, 'Let's face it, we didn't have much in common.' Say, 'We always got on well together but we cannot continue to go on like this. . . .' That last phrase means nothing at all, but it doesn't matter.

If a man wishes to be really gentle his letter might pretend the parting is because of *too much* affection, thus:

It is not because I do not love you. It is because I am *too much* in love with you. I am more in love every day and I am afraid of becoming completely dependent on you. . . .

No intelligent girl will believe this drivel, but it will be a pleasant boost to her ego.

A solicitor I know, in his youth, used to incorporate legal

clauses into his farewell letters, after an unfortunate incident in which a girl sued him for the return of something she gave him. He would write:

I shall miss you terribly, darling. Could you also kindly note that this letter is not meant to imply any admission of liability on my part in any way whatsoever.
    All my love, sweetheart. Goodbye.
    Alistair.

No one but a legal man could stoop that low (except perhaps a journalist).

If the girl breaks off an affair it should never be allowed to pass without a letter of reply. This is not politeness, just the chance for getting some sort of revenge. I always think of a letter Askew wrote after being jilted in particularly distressing circumstances. He spent two whole pages saying how pleased he was the girl had found happiness and concluded in a highly formal manner:

I shall always think of you with pleasure. In conclusion allow me to congratulate you, Dorothy, on being one of the finest exponents of the *soixante-neuf* it has been my privilege to meet. Do by all means show this letter to your new boyfriend if you wish.
I have the honour to be madam,
    Your obedient servant
      J. Askew M. I. Mech. E.

Leaving aside lunatic communications of this nature, the sort of reply to a woman's farewell letter must depend on circumstances. If one has been badly treated, one is justified in firing a parting shot. But never admit to having been hurt – three pages of bitterness will only reveal how much the girl has wounded you and being only human she will feel a certain sense of power. Never appeal to a woman's morality – they have none. Nobody has where a break-up is concerned. Don't try to contrast your doggy faithfulness with her goings-on. If parting in anger, the best farewell is a letter which suggests you never cared a damn anyway. I know this, because a girl sent a letter like that and I was deeply wounded. Here it is:

Dear Mike,

Thanks for your letter. I'm glad you wrote because I was getting completely bored with the whole thing and had intended to tell you myself, only I didn't want to hurt your ego, which I know is a little sensitive in regard to women, as with most men of your age. It was about time we split up anyway and thanks for making the first move. Good luck and give me a ring sometime, but not on Saturday as I shall not be sleeping at home.

Sincerely,

Beryl

What a superb piece of writing. Note the cunning phrase at the end: 'I shall not be sleeping at home.' Immediately jealousies arise. Was she carrying on with someone else all the time? I commend this letter to Coarse Lovers of both sexes as the perfect model for replying to a letter of rejection. My obvious reaction was to wish I hadn't broken off the affair. I still wish I hadn't. How dare she. . . .

One difficulty with a goodbye letter is that, being written under stress, it may not be very clear. I remember receiving one from a girl which was so emotional I quite mistook its purpose. It went something like:

Oh God, Mike, I feel so rotten about this, I just don't know where I am. This is *not* a Dear John letter [*usually a sign that it is*], it's just that I am so mixed up. I suppose in some ways I have never really grown up and don't know my own mind but I know you'll understand as you've always been kind although I didn't always appreciate it. I feel I desperately need help. Don't be too hard on me.

All my love, Jane.

When I got this extraordinary missive, I was touched. She obviously needed me. This was a cry for help. How unkind I had been to suspect her of being less affectionate recently. I immediately went round to her house. She opened the door and said, rather coldly I thought, 'Hullo Mike. What do you want?' As she spoke I saw a large man wearing no shirt and with egg stains down the front of his vest coming down the stairs and going up again when he saw me.

'I've come to help you,' I said.

'Help me? Why should you want to help me?'

'Well, you said in your letter. . . .'

'Oh that. I didn't really say that, did I? I must have been pissed. Well, actually it's a bit difficult for you to come in now because I've got a visitor but why don't you give me a ring at the office sometime, eh? I've got to run now because we're going to the cinema, but just ring me any time you like. You know I'm always glad to hear from you. . . .'

I slunk away, feeling rather like someone who thought he'd won the National Lottery and then found he'd lost the ticket.

A useful wheeze in writing farewell is to capitalize on the fact that women often have a pitiful belief in astrology and tend to blame the stars for everything. 'Just the sort of rotten trick you would expect from a Scorpio,' they'll say. A man could write, therefore, some phrase about 'feeling we have to part because we Capricorns just can't conduct long-term relationships . . .' and it would be accepted as a perfectly logical and inoffensive explanation.

It sometimes happens that both of a pair who are separating are deeply involved in some local organization. It is desperately difficult not to allow the split to spill over into this area, especially if the third leg of a triangle is also a member. For years I sat on a sub-committee of an amateur theatre and there were just three of us – myself, a girl and another man. The other two-thirds of the committee were sleeping together so I could never get my views accepted until they split up, after which a radical policy change was made and, apart from introducing a totally new theatrical concept, the girl and I became partners.

Alas, the affair spilled over into the annual meeting with the man shouting at the girl, 'How can anyone as frigid as you want to do a D. H. Lawrence play?' and the chairman frantically telling the secretary, 'Don't put that in the minutes.' Fortunately some of it did get in, with the result that part of the minutes read like the third chapter of *Lady Chatterley's*

Lover. People still sneak a look at the committee files to read the debate on the report of the play selection sub-committee:

After Mr Johnson had alleged that the secretary of the play selection sub-committee was frigid, it was resolved not to do a D. H. Lawrence play next year. Mr Green asked for his dissenting vote to be minuted as he did not personally find the sub-committee secretary frigid, although he could well believe Mr Johnson could not satisfy anyone. Mr Johnson rose on a point of order and said it was well-known that Mr Green had a tool like an over-ripe banana. At this point the chairman declared the matter closed. . . .

Never resign over this sort of thing. It may be difficult to get back. Just lie low for three or four months, sending your apologies for absence and the whole thing will blow over. And don't be put off a similar affair. I do not believe in the old moral about not fouling your own doorstep. That is where most of the girls are. I always suspect that particular motto is used as a rationalization by people who rather wish they had indeed fouled the local doorstep, but never had the courage.

Once a separation has taken place, it is important to soften the sense of loss which occurs, even when the parting was your idea. The wronged party, of course, will have suffered a blow to their ego as well. It is necessary to convince yourself you were in the right. Some useful ways of rationalizing the situation are summed up in the following comfort-phrases, which can be repeated over and over again to yourself, to friends, or anyone who will listen. When talking to another person it is more effective if each phrase is prefaced by the words, 'Between you, me and the gatepost, old man. . . .'
'I never really enjoyed it anyway.'
'She never really enjoyed it anyway.'
'Her demands were insatiable.'
'She was absolutely frigid.'
'She didn't know what she wanted.'
'She knew what she wanted and nothing was going to stop her.'
'She never wanted a man.'
'She wanted every man.'

'I'm happier on my own.'

'She's happier on her own.'

'Those big-chested girls often turn to fat.'

Various permutations can be rung on the above according to individual taste. Avoid the truth at all costs.

Be careful from whom you seek comfort and help after a break-up. One of the worst horrors of ending an affair is the so-called assistance from well-meaning people which twists the knife in the wound. I am thinking of friends who insist on saying how they all knew you were being treated badly but couldn't do anything about it (it's just about the last straw to discover everyone knew you were being deceived except yourself). Or people who urge you to snap out of it. Or those who say they sympathize deeply because their own love life has always been so happy and they couldn't stand it if Cynthia left them, 'No, I think I'd shoot myself if Cynthia treated me the way Margaret treated you. . . .'

Parents can be among the worst Job's comforters, especially if they are elderly or naïve, since they frequently have no conception of what the real situation is. When my old pal Watkins was jilted by a girl he adored he took me down to spend a weekend with his elderly mother at Hastings, the idea being to Forget It All for a few days. Alas, poor Watkins sat staring into space and pouring whisky absentmindedly into his ear while his old mother, thinking to comfort him, tweeted on endlessly about 'how fickle these young girls are today'.

Every word was like a fresh stab to poor Watkins's heart. 'Never you mind dear,' she droned on. 'I'm sorry your little flirtation is over but you probably don't know much about girls at your age,' (he was in fact thirty-five and had made love to just about anything that moved in the district). 'I know how changeable young girls can be. It's because they like to tease the boys a little. . . .'

At this I thought Watkins would explode because his former love had indeed liked to tease him a little by blowing with her warm, sweet-scented breath upon his sensitive parts. But he could hardly confide that to his old mother and he had to sit there hour after hour while she poured forth her hopes that he would meet a good girl, not one of these fast young things but a decent girl who would mend his clothes for him.

By all means drink for comfort in a separation *but don't do it in public*. It's fatal to go into a bar and start knocking back gin to make you feel better because by ten o'clock you'll be blubbering. I shall never forget Askew, after one of his many shattered affairs, drinking so much that he sobbed all over the local pub and everybody else started to feel miserable too. Some of the women were in tears. Eventually the manager asked him to leave 'because the noise of your grief is affecting trade'.

At the time of parting a difference between the sexes shows itself. Women seem to be able to forget much more quickly than men. Nature seems to urge them to obliterate the memory of that little twit and get on with the next affair as soon as possible. Men live more in the past. They also have a pathetic belief that, if a girl gives way to their wishes once, she will always be willing to oblige on a future occasion. Askew has been known to call upon a former girlfriend after not seeing her for three years and expect to make love there and then. 'I can't understand what's got into the girl,' he says when refused.

There is a final social ritual concerned with splitting-up. When a girl gets married or has a new boyfriend, she invites her former partner round for a meal with them both and, if he wishes, he can bring *his* new partner. This is a ceremony of staking out social territory, the human equivalent of the way dogs pee on lamp-posts to mark their boundaries. This especially applies if the parties concerned are from the same small social group, such as a tennis club or drama society.

And in the end, of course, the only cure for a broken heart is a new affair. Ever-optimistic, the Coarse Lover sets out once again on the uncharted seas, with the eternal hope of all Coarse sportsmen – that this time it will all be all right.

Appendix

Glossary of Commony Used Male Sexual Phrases and Their
True Meanings

Believe me, the women just flocked round. . . .	He ogled them as they passed by
They were all for it. . . .	He managed to get near one and touch her bottom
Those air stewardesses are randy as hell. . . .	They gave him that plastic artificial smile
I was just about flaked out by now, but. . . .	He was impotent
If I'd played my cards right. . . .	He was scared stiff
Believe me, I can get as much as I want. . . .	He doesn't get any
She was a nymphomaniac. . . .	He wasn't' much good
I never really enjoyed it. . . .	She never really enjoyed it
Of course Freda's always been a good wife to me. . . .	Yes, but he went off her about twenty years ago

As you get older you don't bother much about sex. . . .	He hasn't any choice
I reckon my sexual performance is the same as anybody else's. . . .	He is worried that it isn't
There's a little girl who works in the corner shop who'd do anything for me. . . .	She doesn't even know his name
You'll be all right there, mate. . . .	You won't
Well, I'm afraid we must be going, it's a long drive. . . .	Tonight's the night
It's a much over-rated pastime. . . .	He wishes he was better at it